Poveglia, a small island in the Venetian lagoon,
has been uninhabited since 1968.
Located between Venice and Lido,
with its ruined hospital and plague burial grounds
has been often described as one of the world's
most haunted places.
Its dark, derelict and forbidding shores
are only minutes away from the city,
but the island remains deserted
and off-limits to the public.
Very few Venetians are prepared
to talk about the island or answer questions.

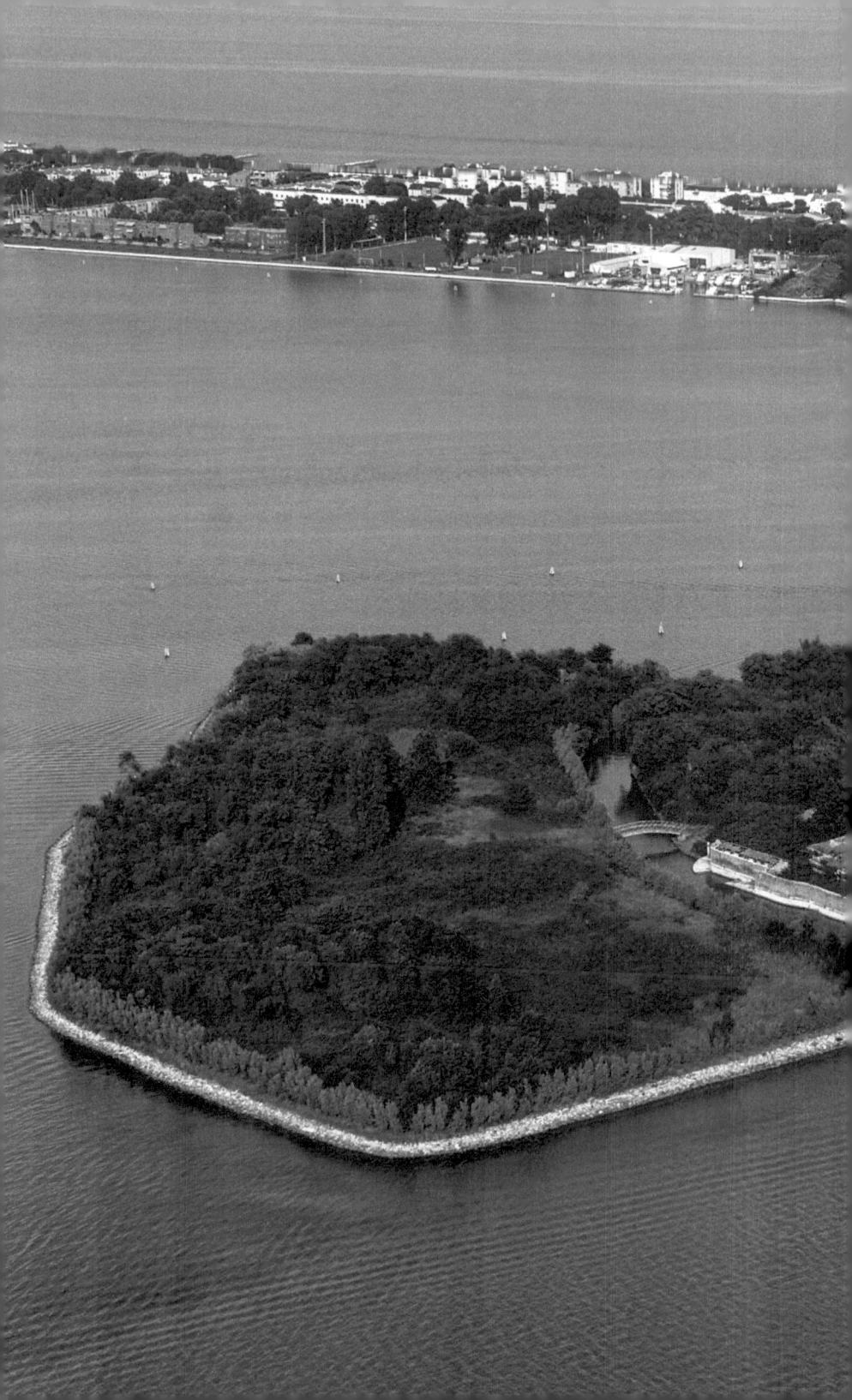

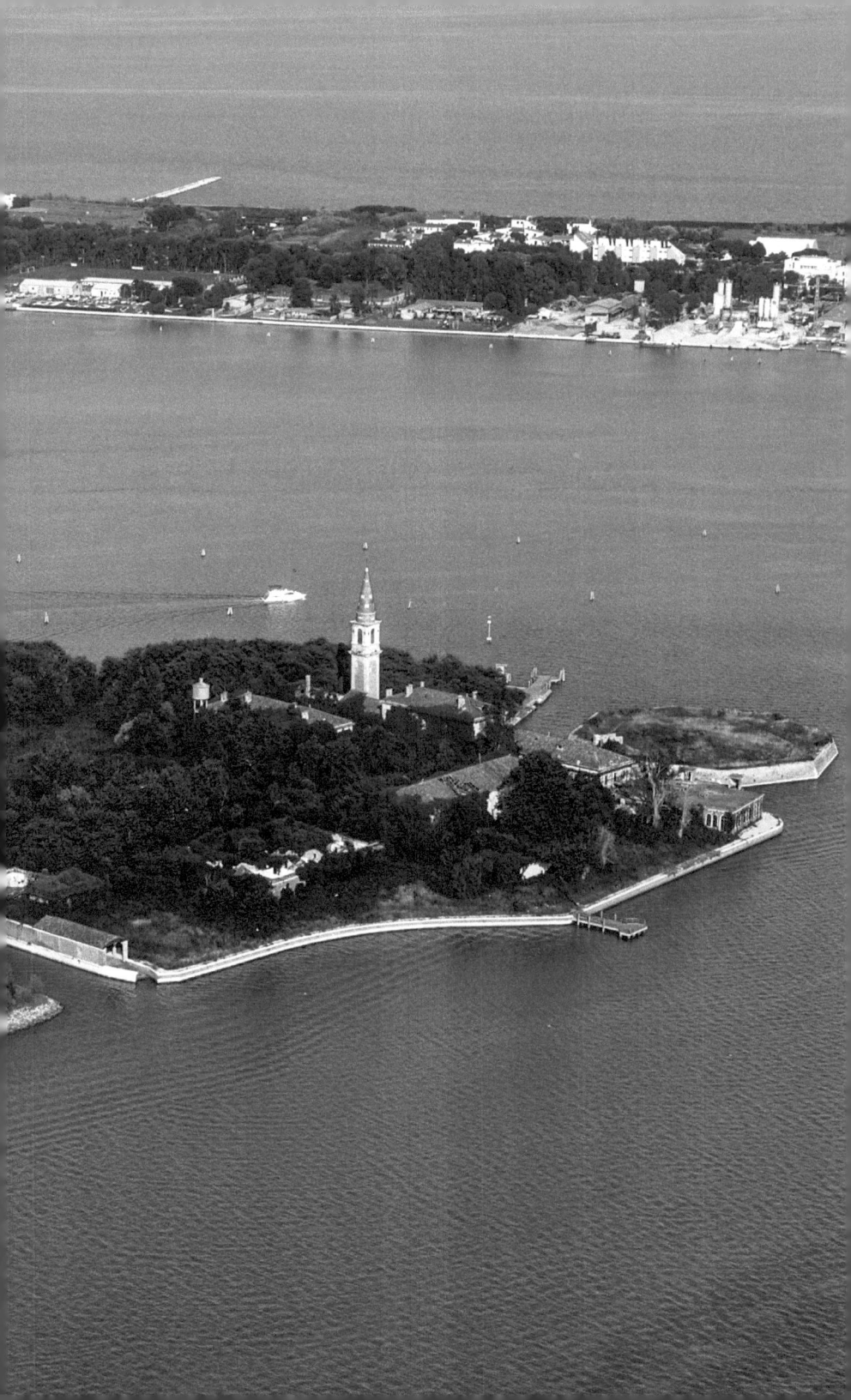

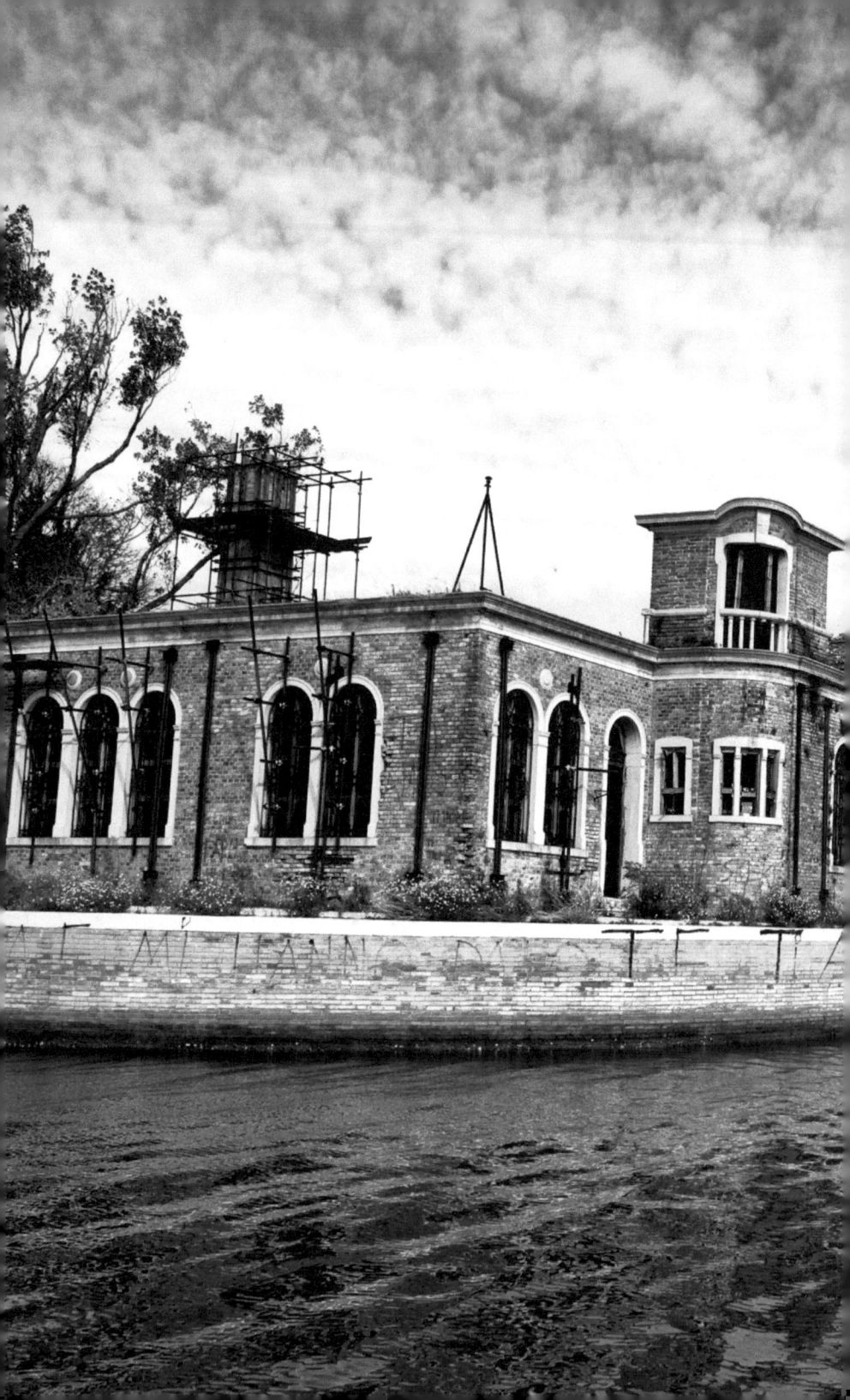

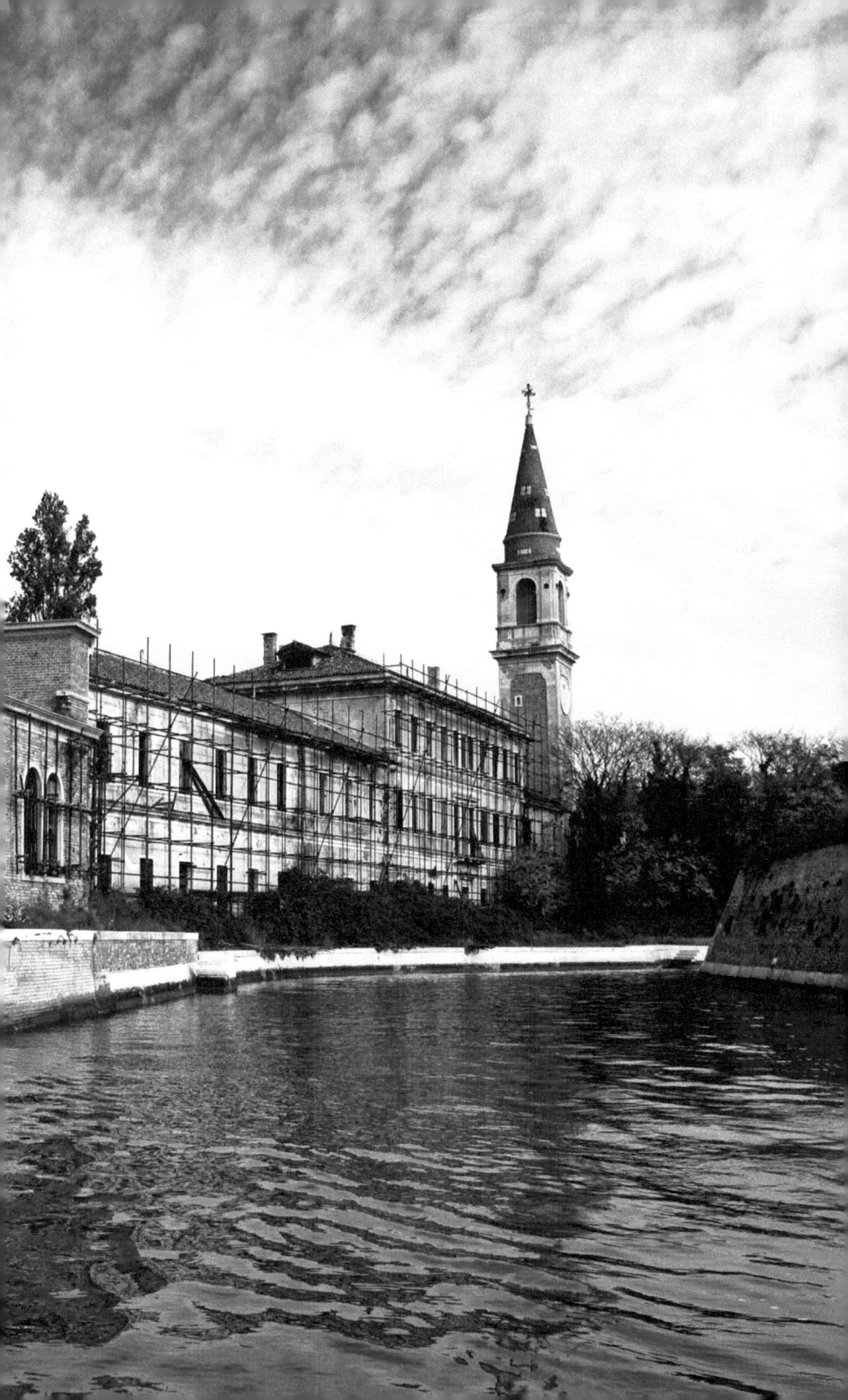

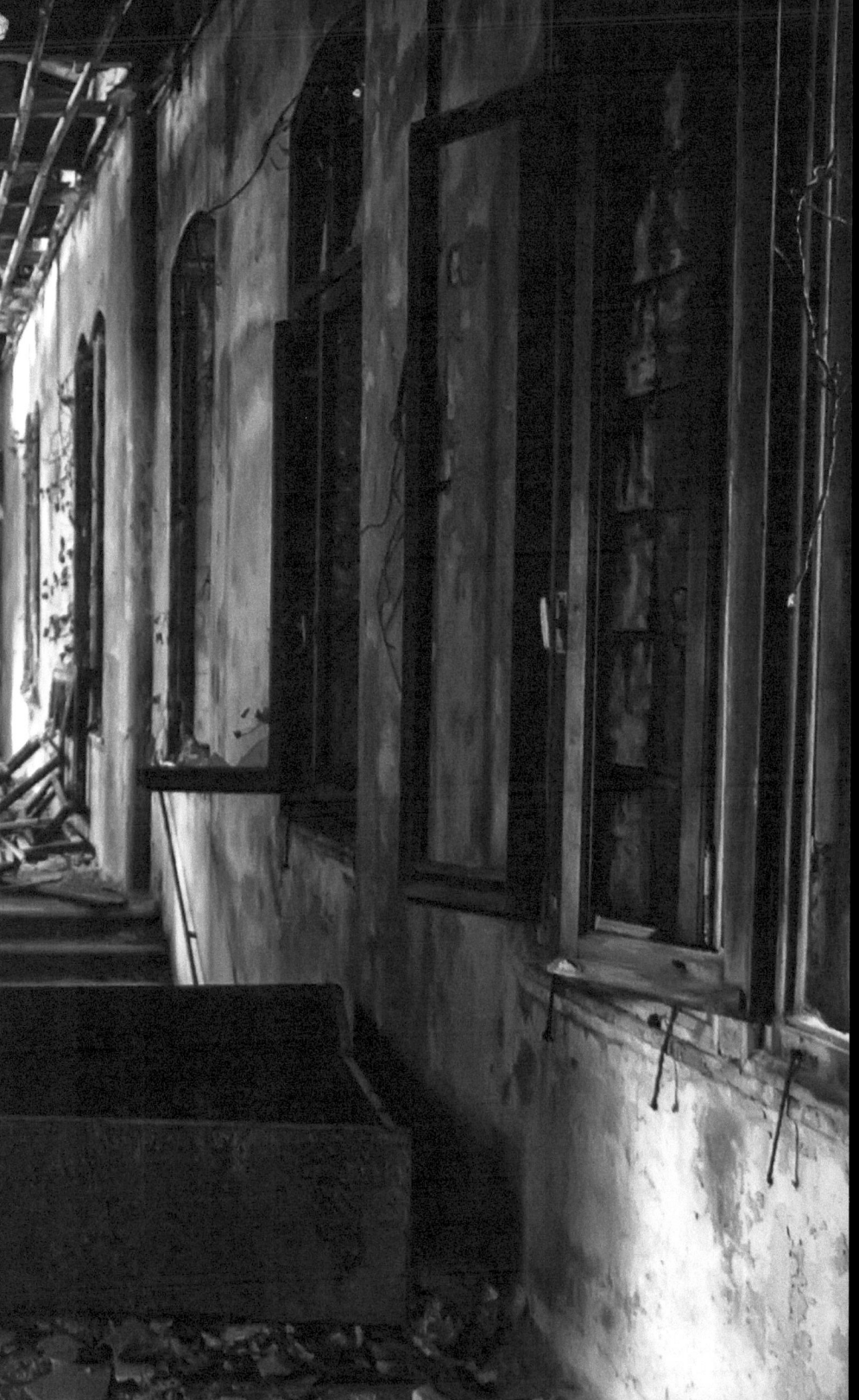

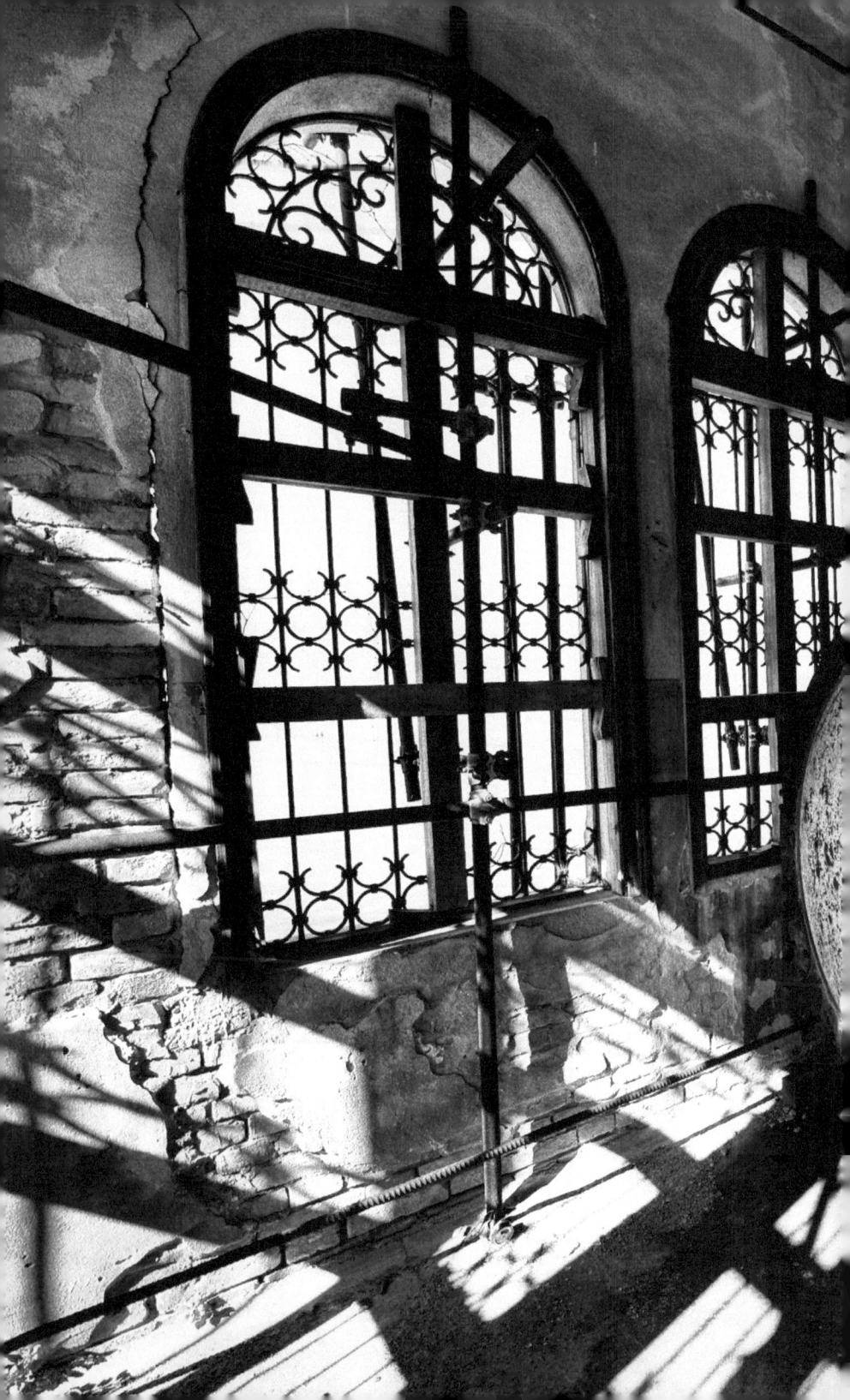

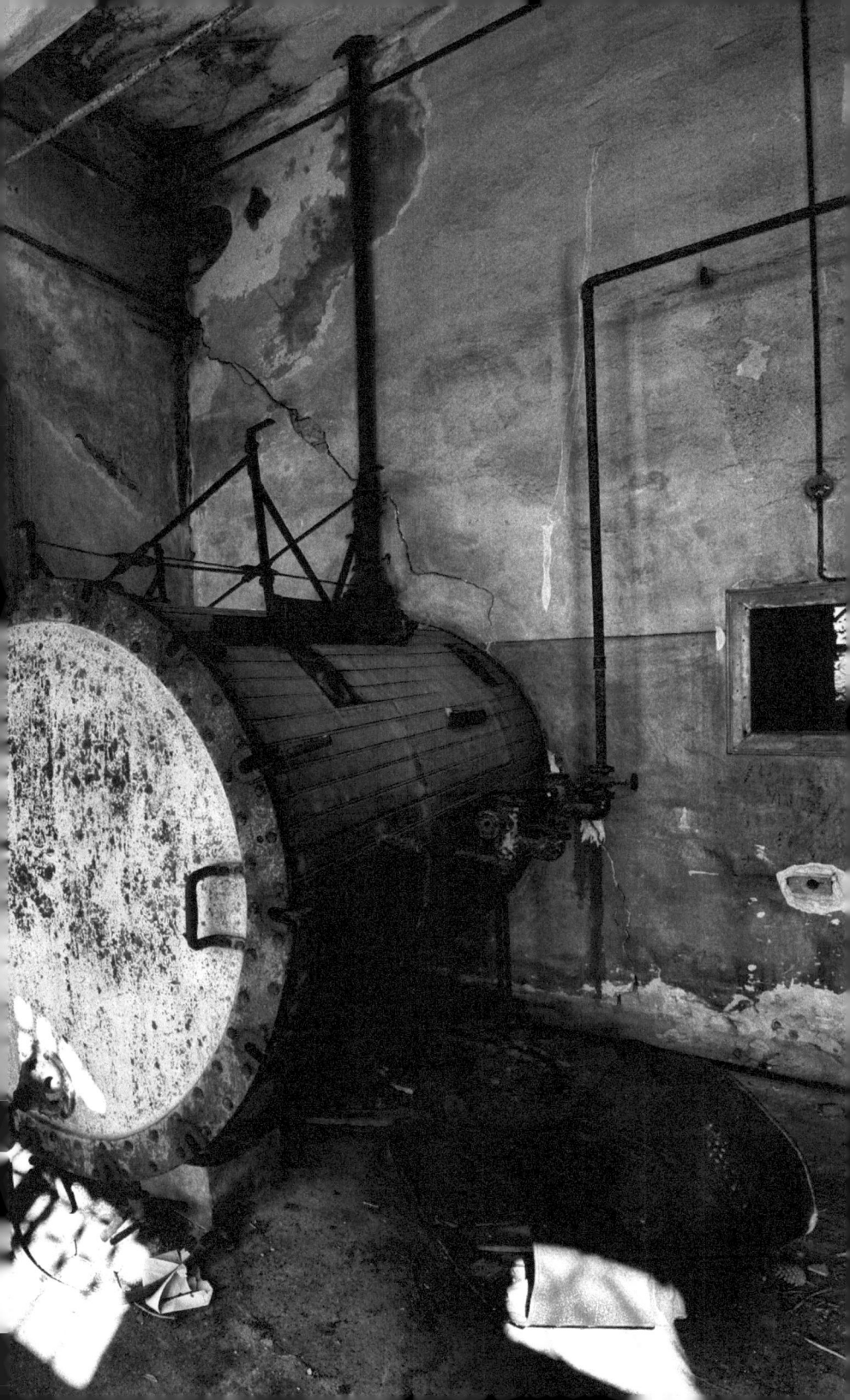

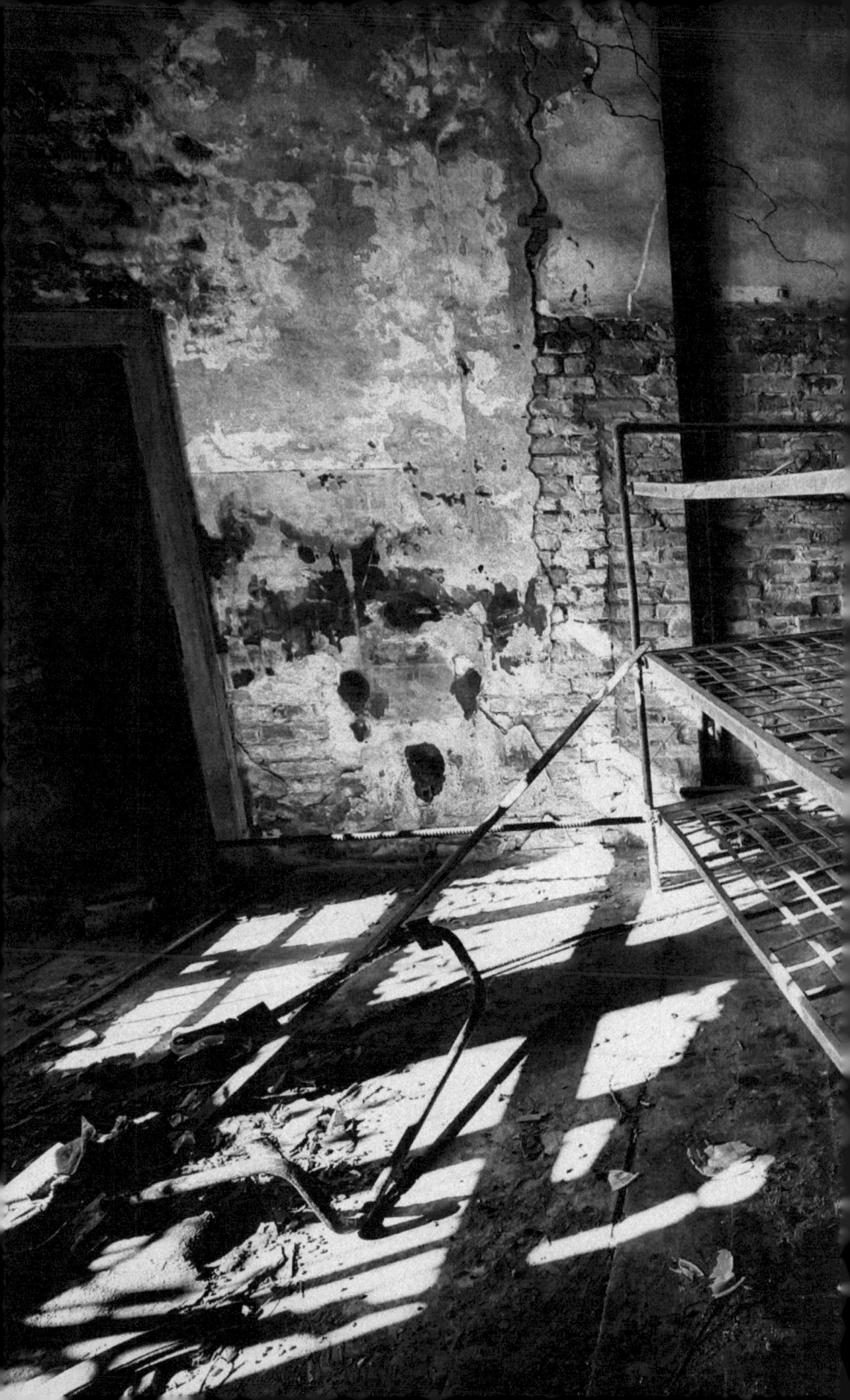

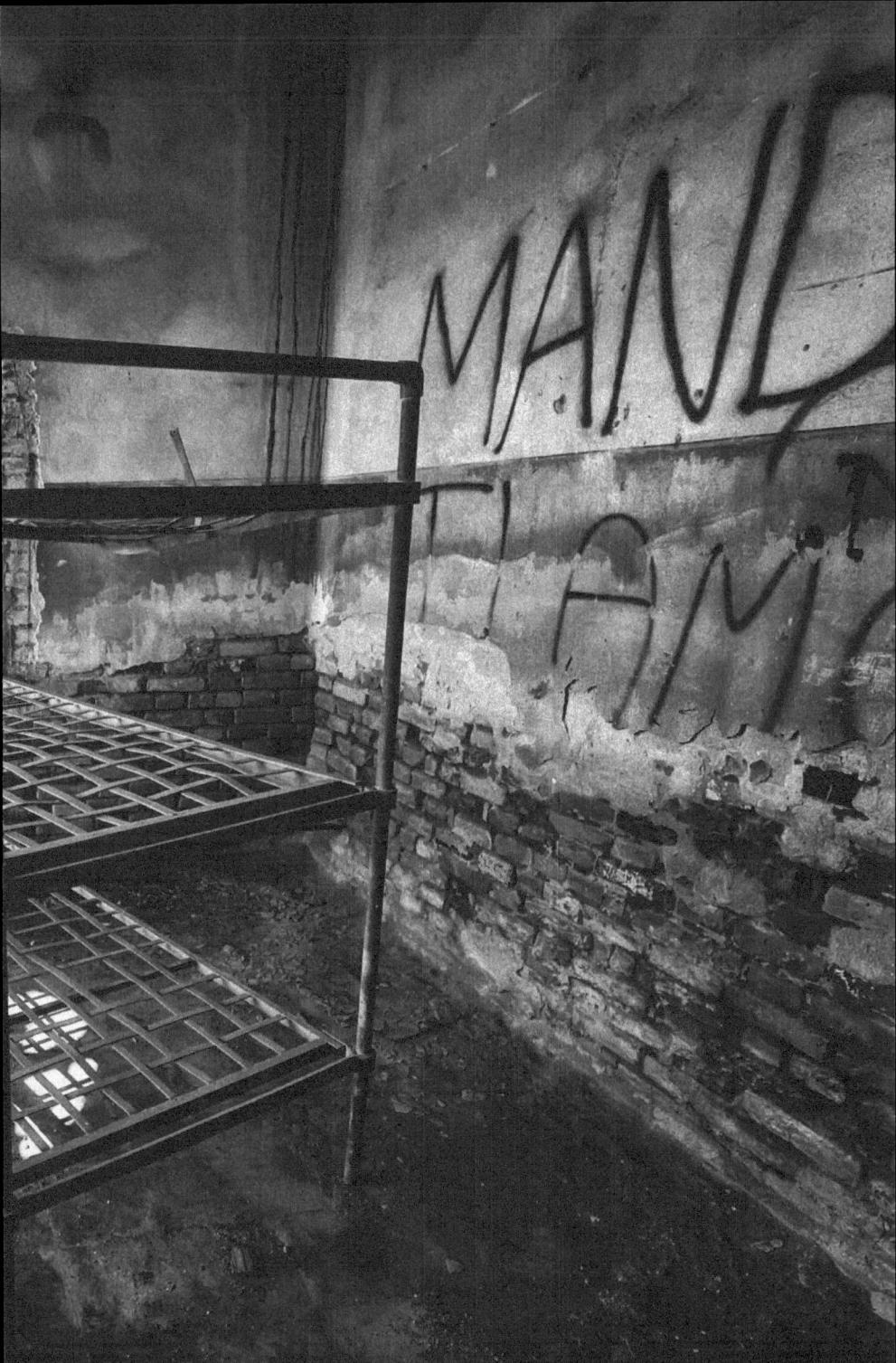

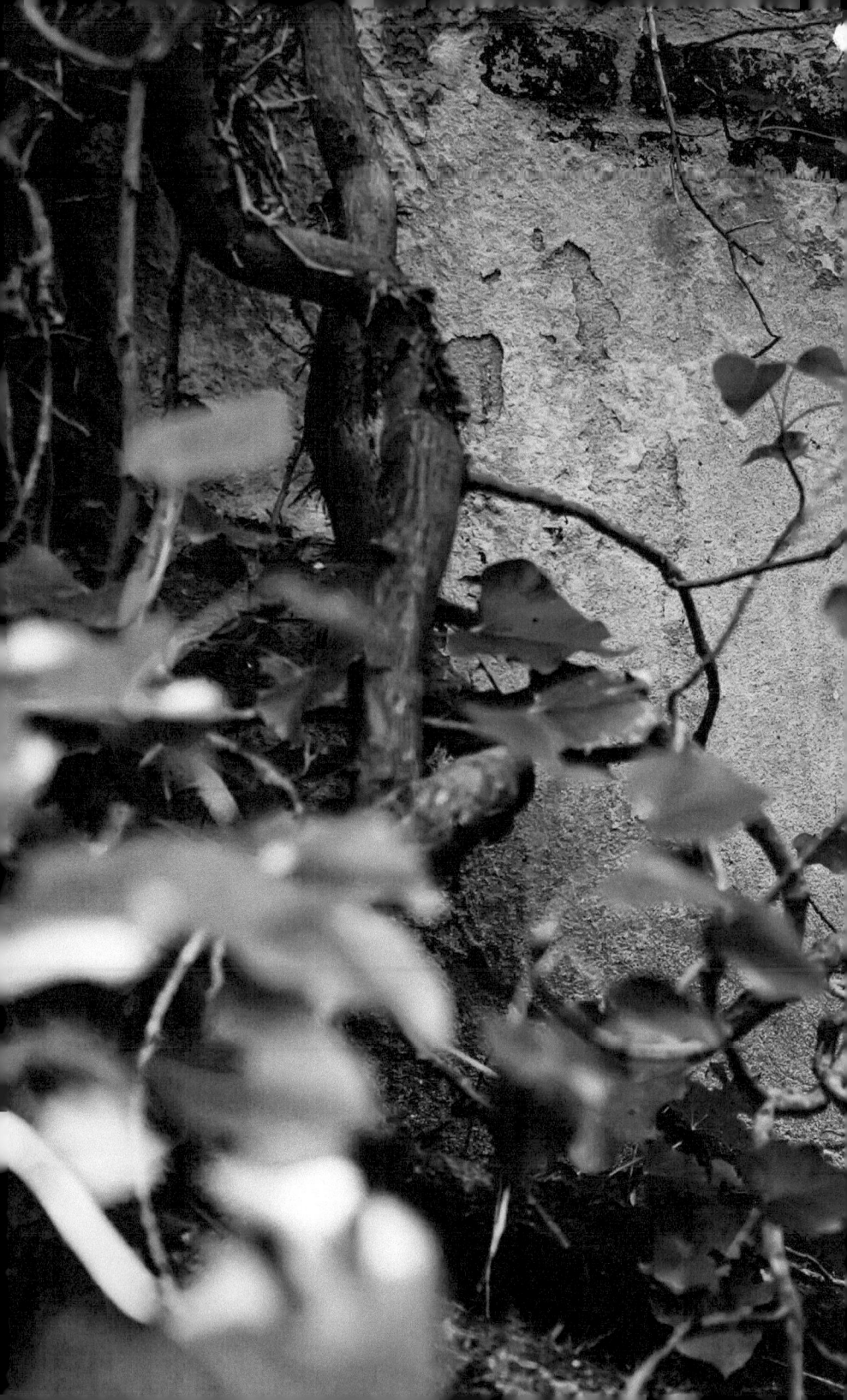

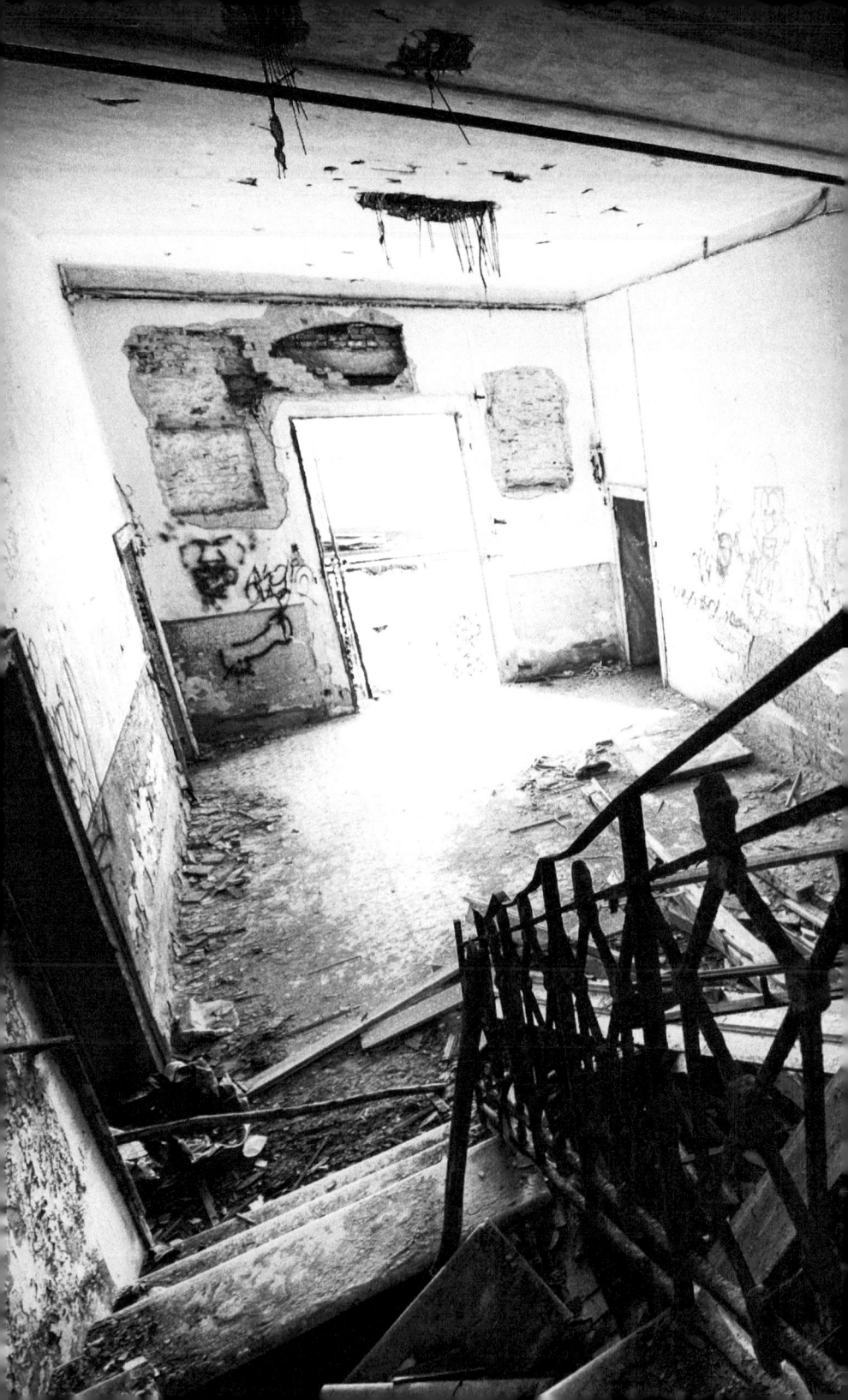

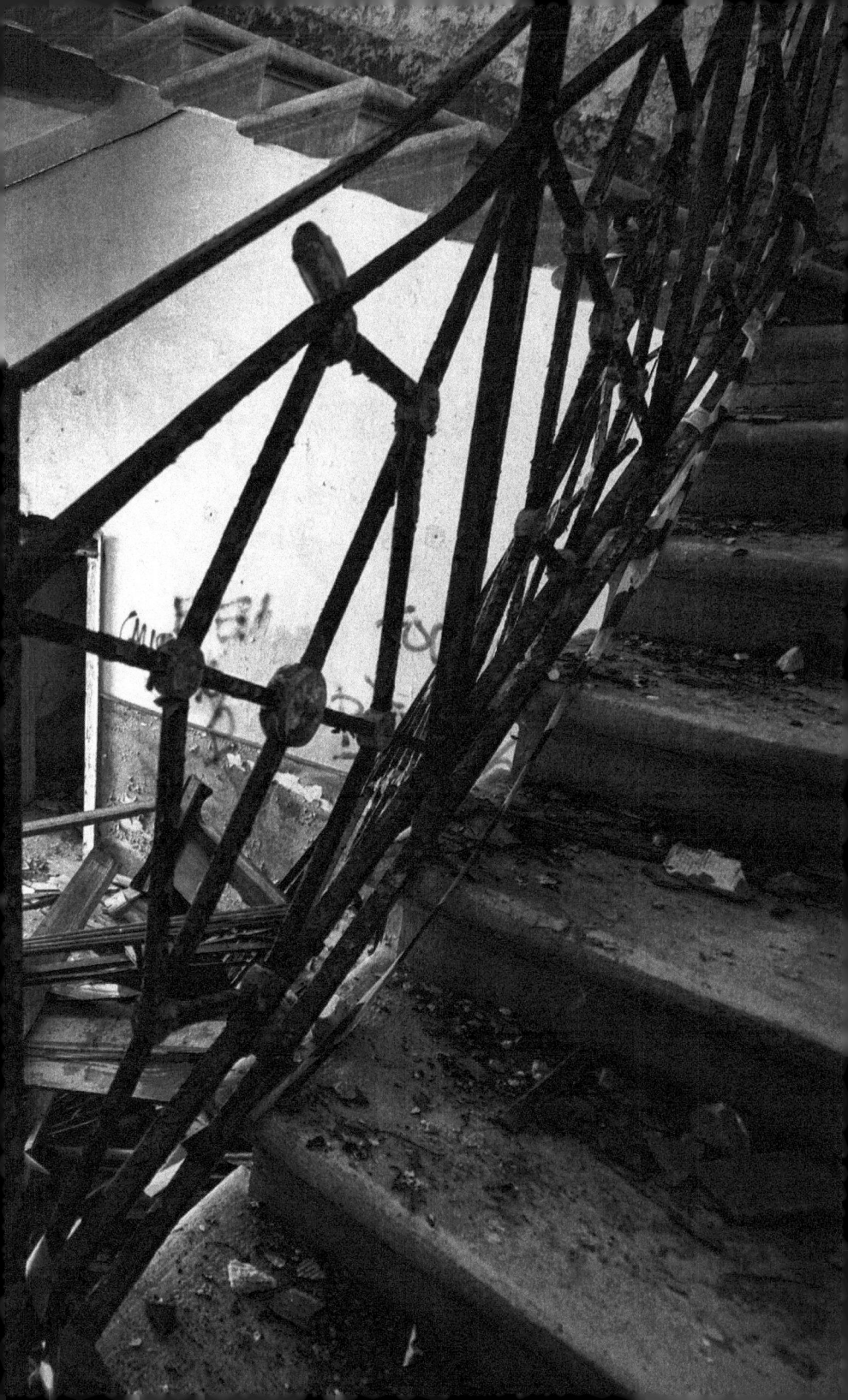

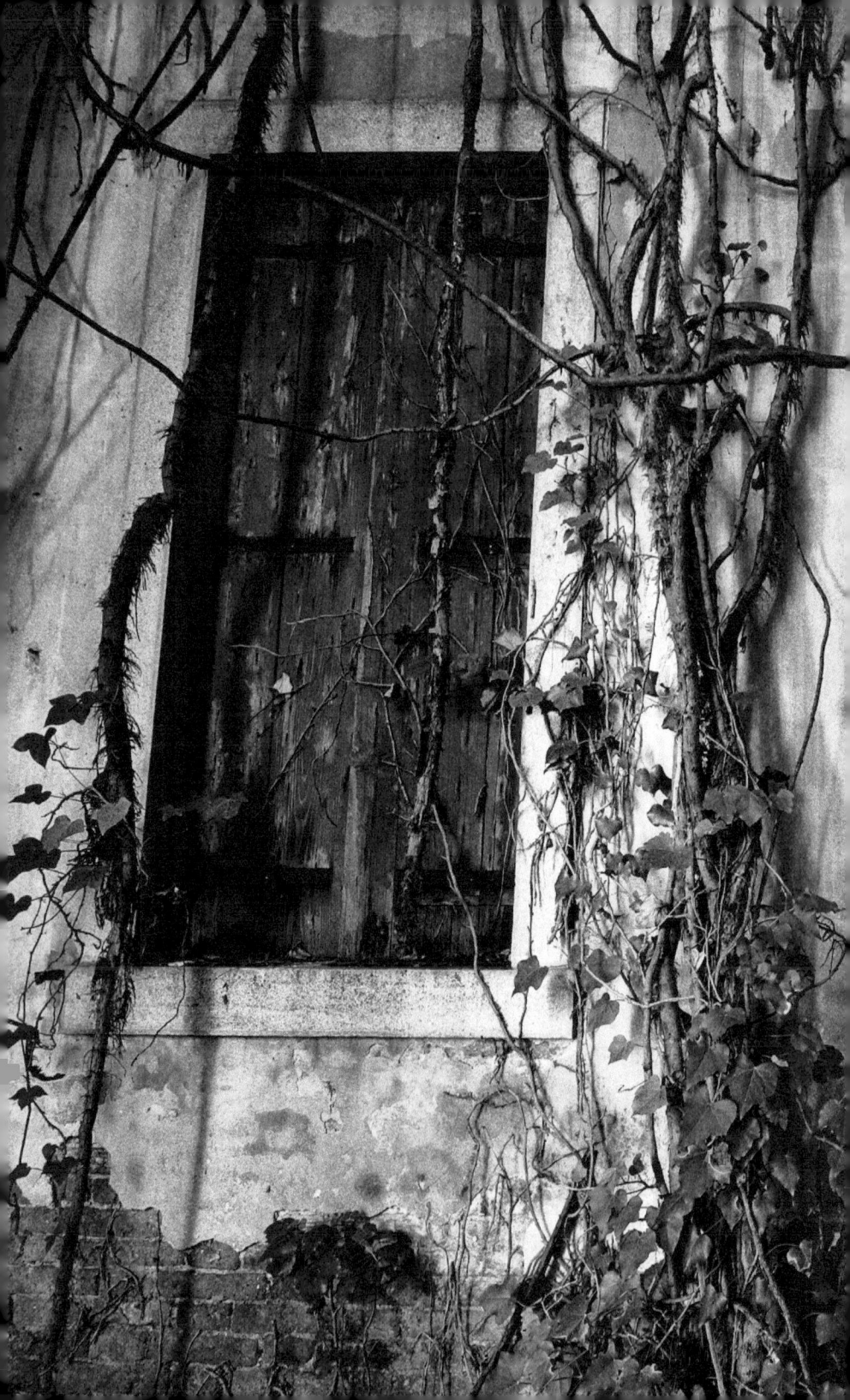

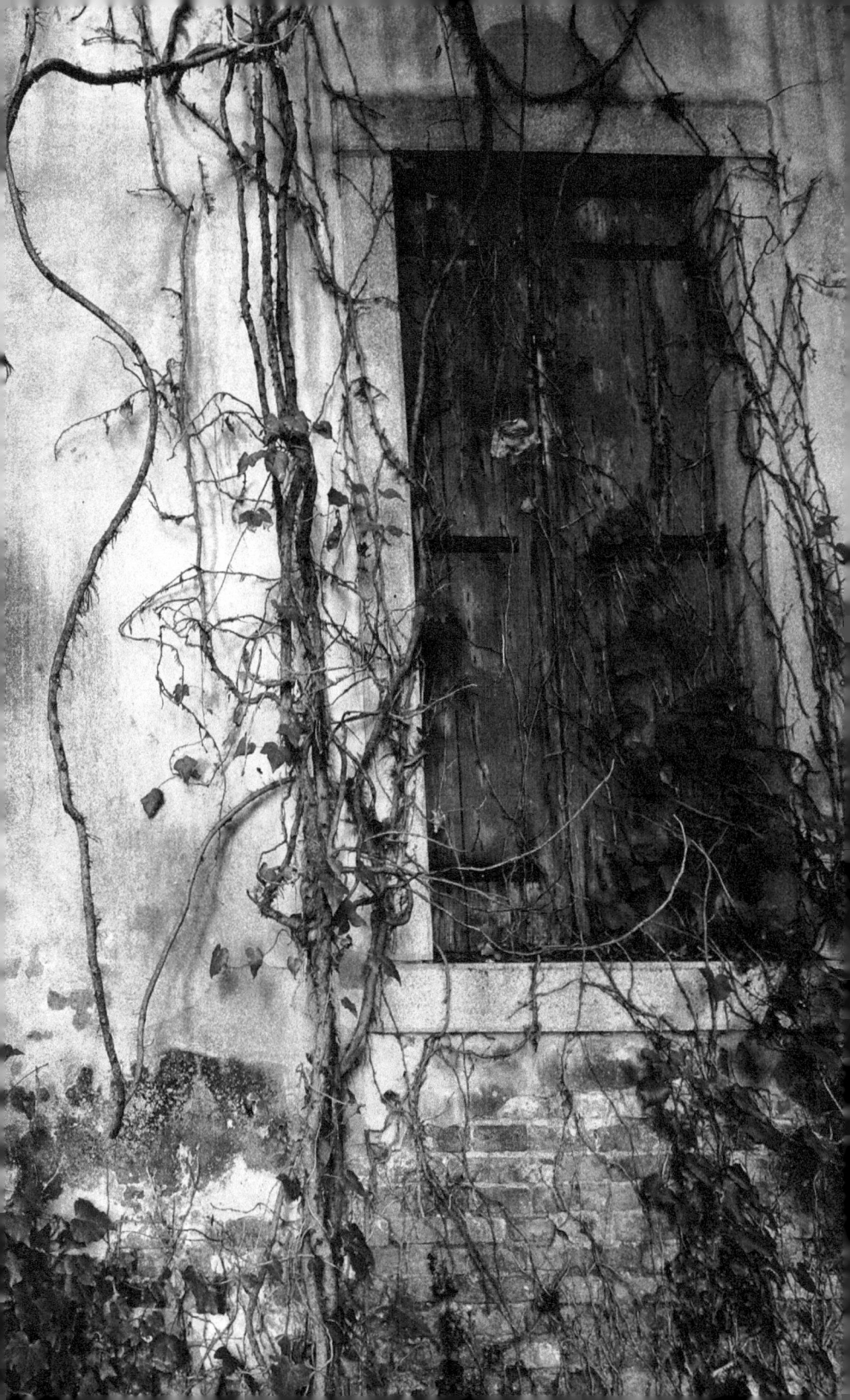

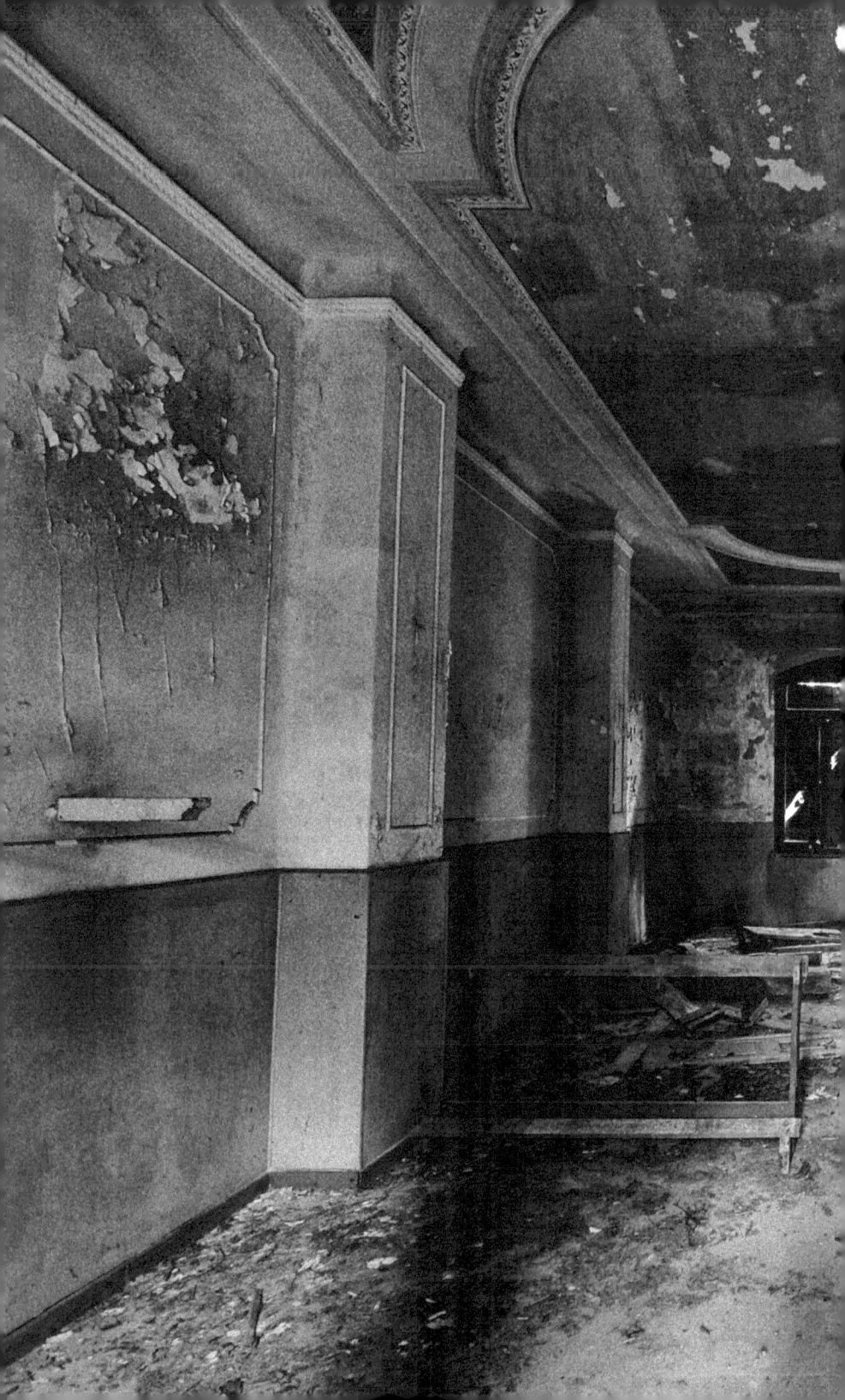

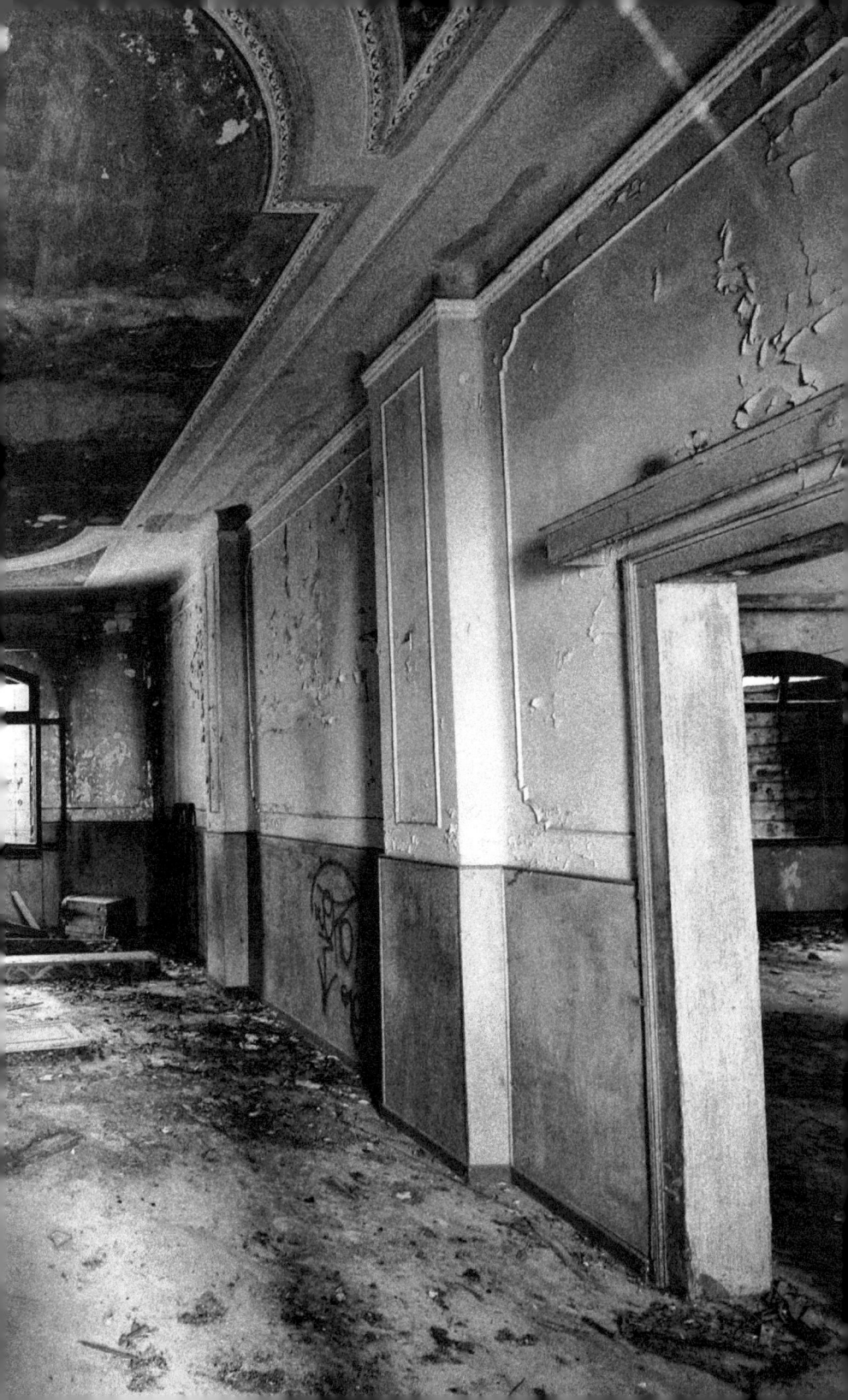

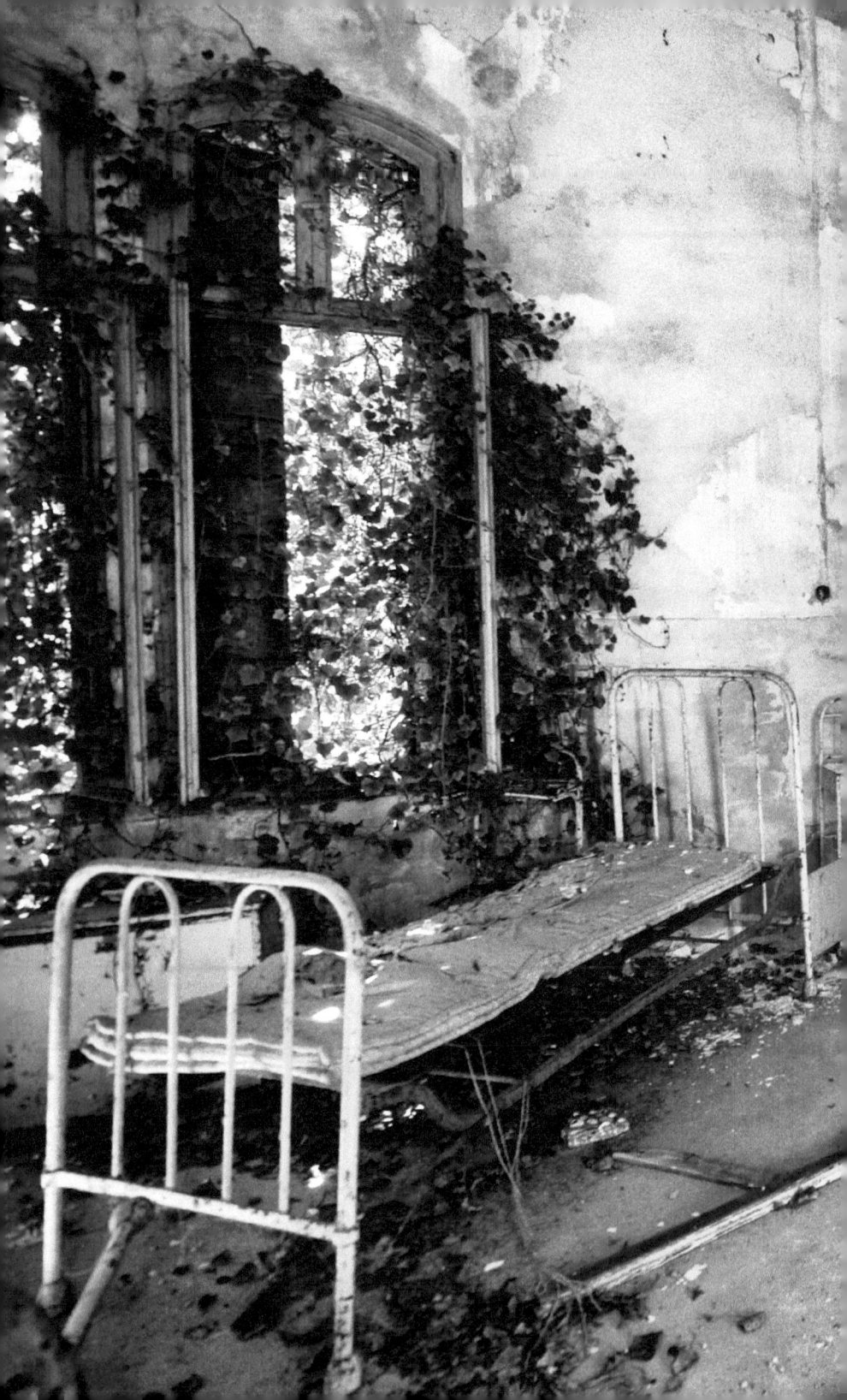

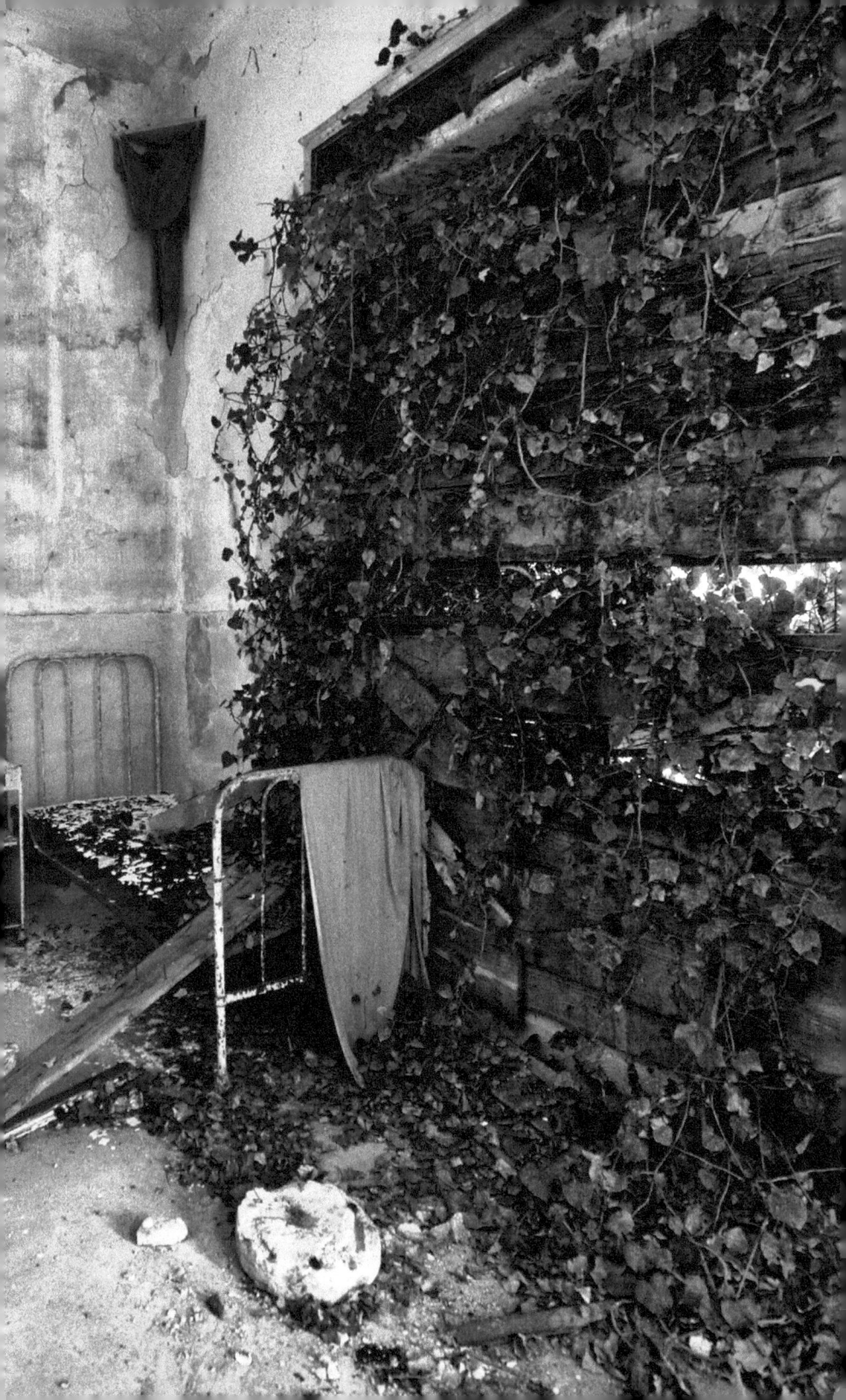

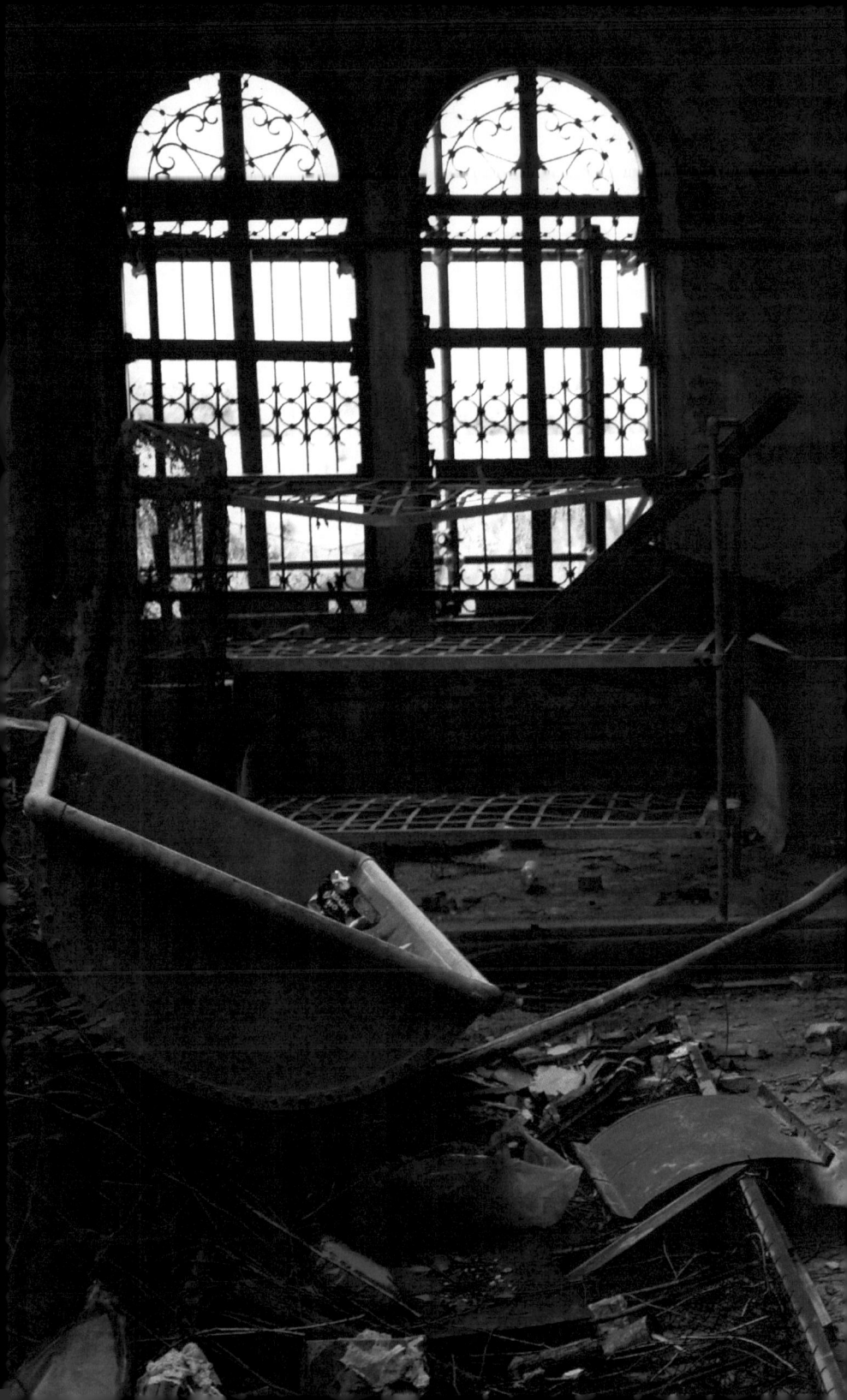

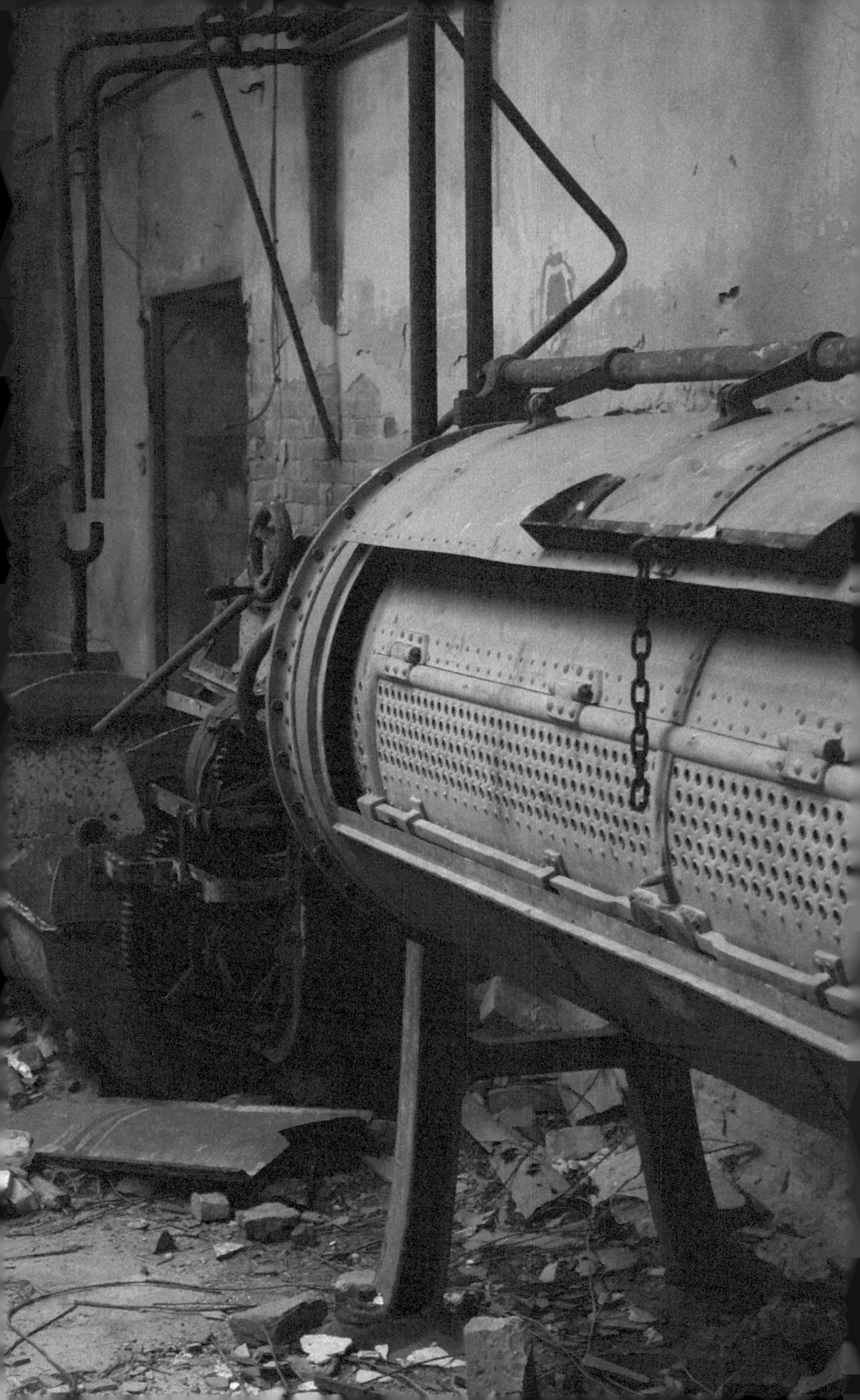

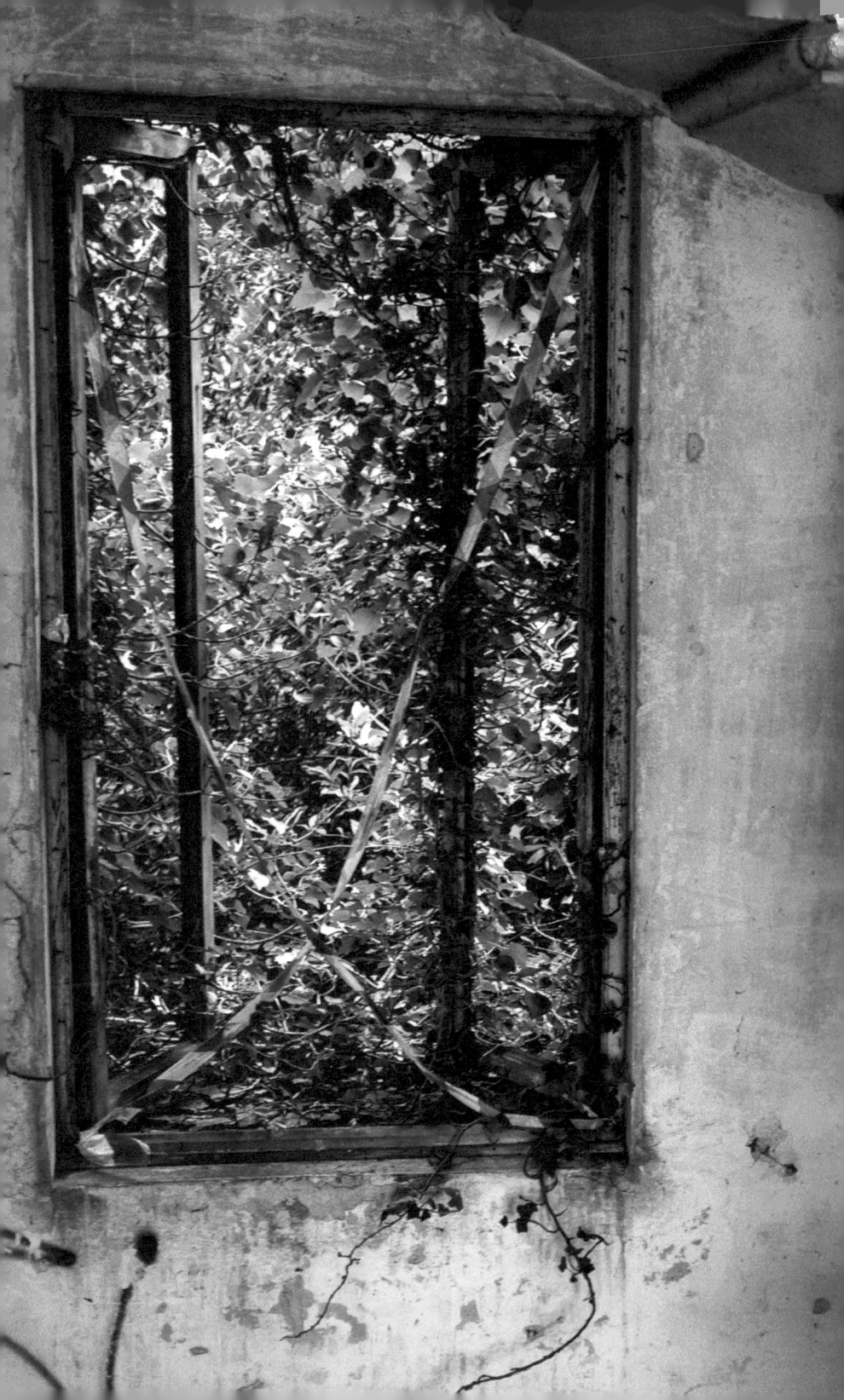

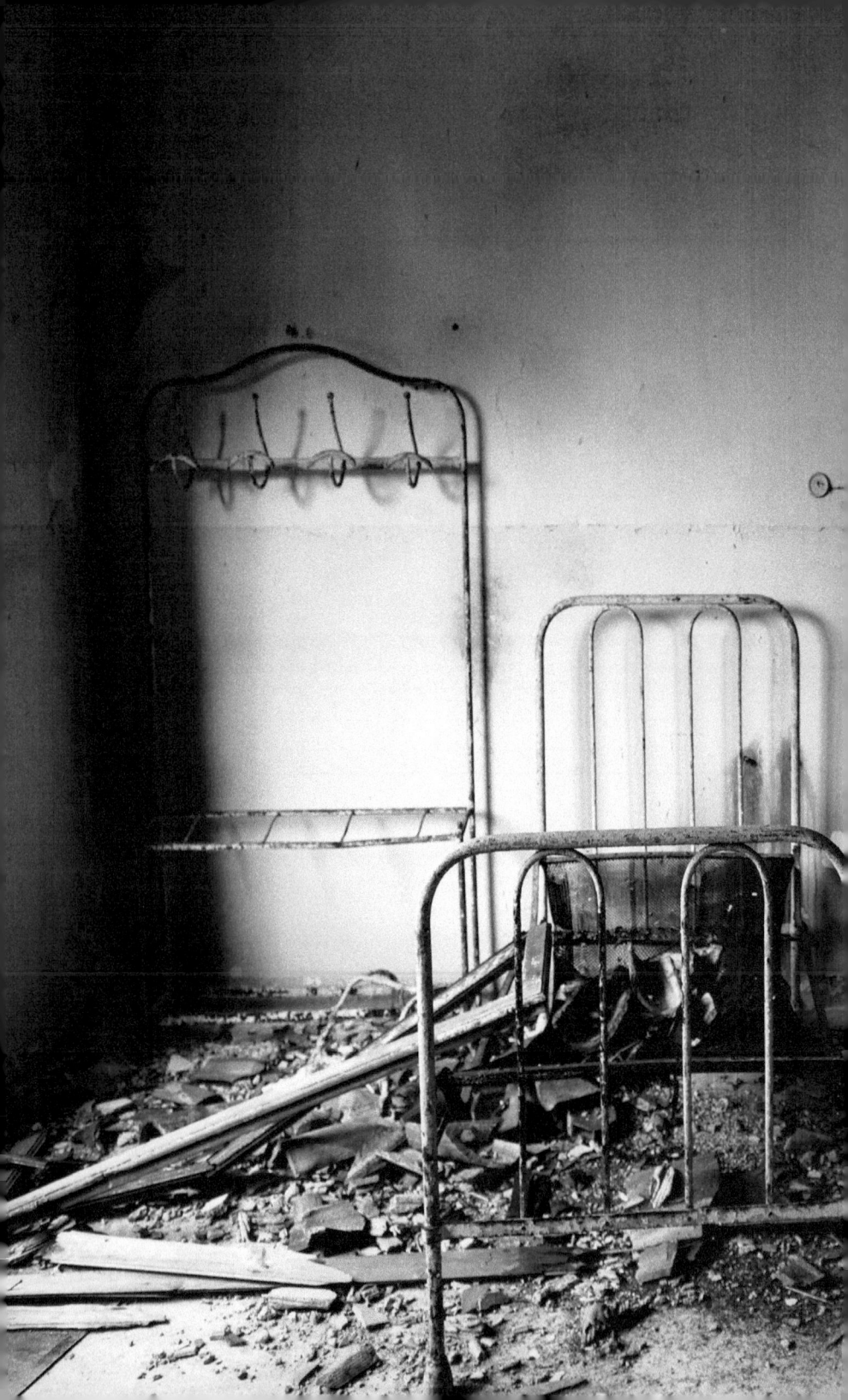

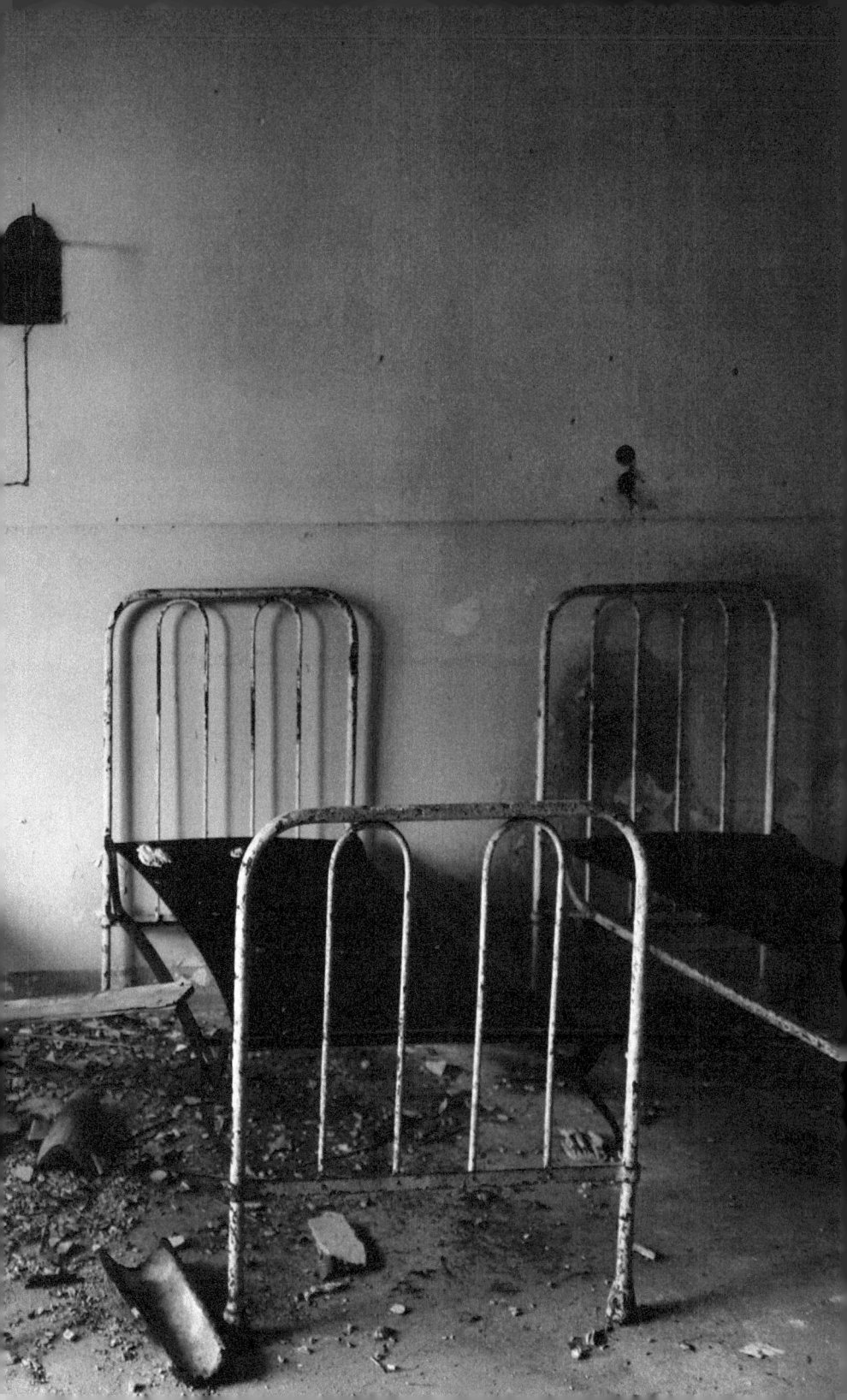

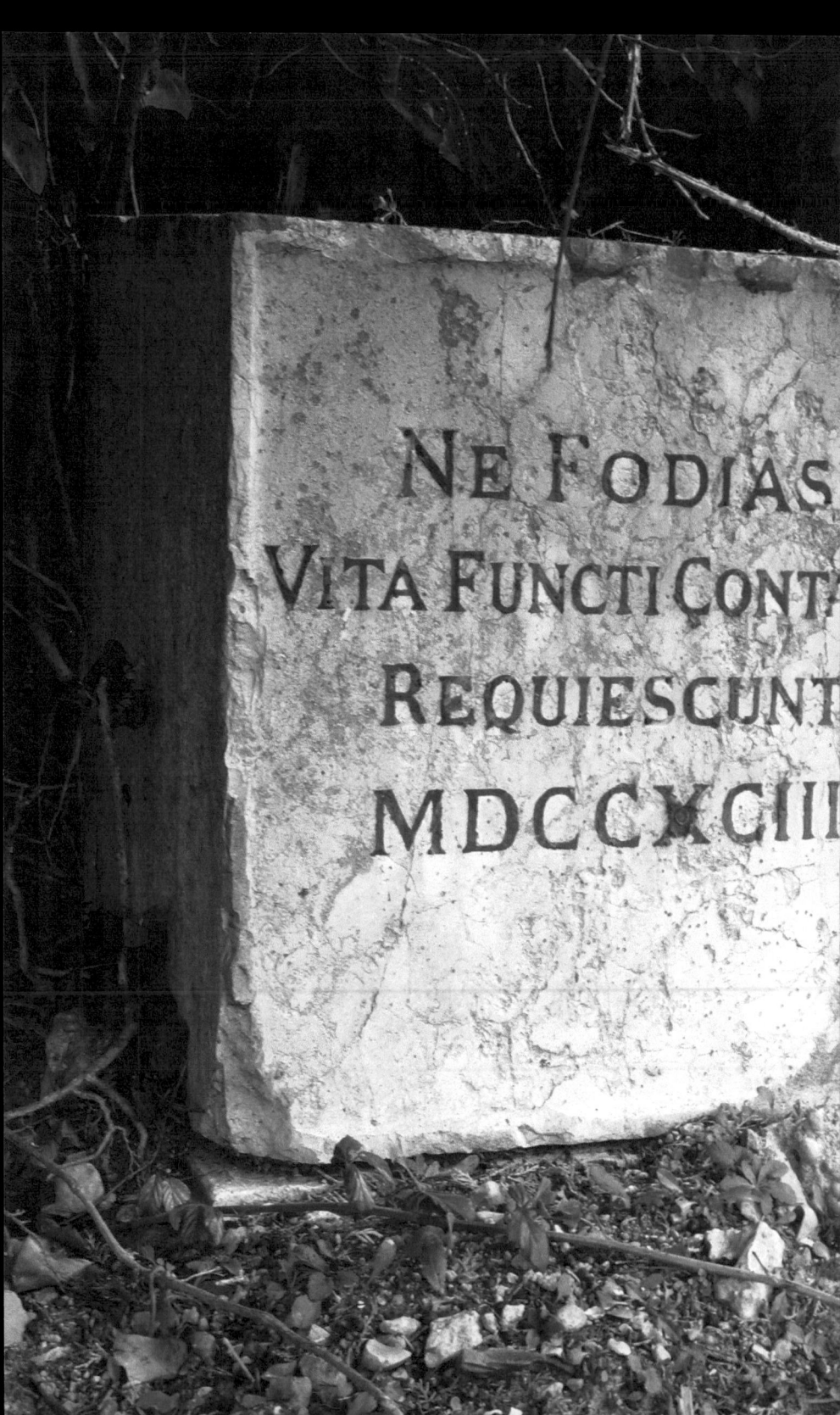

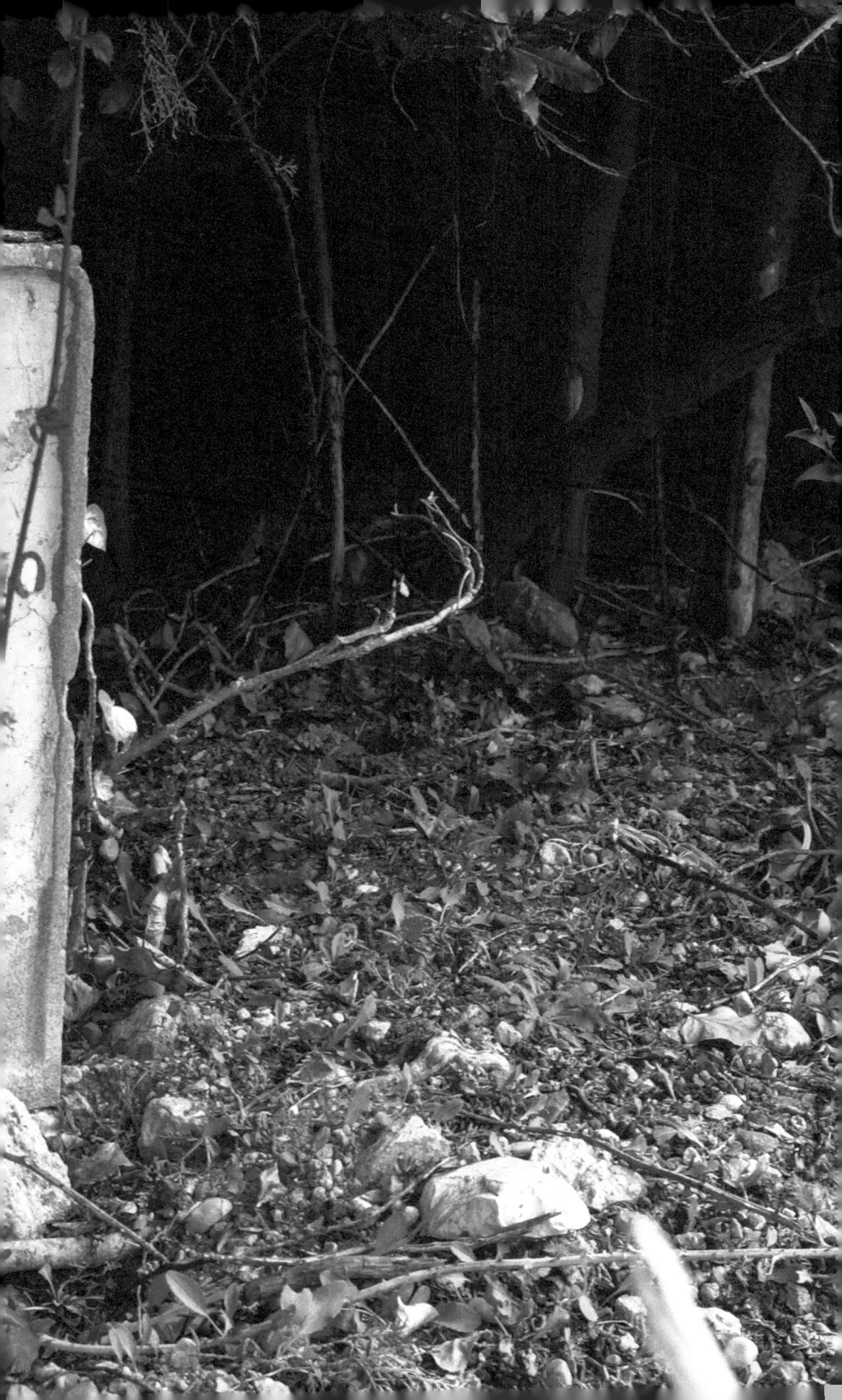

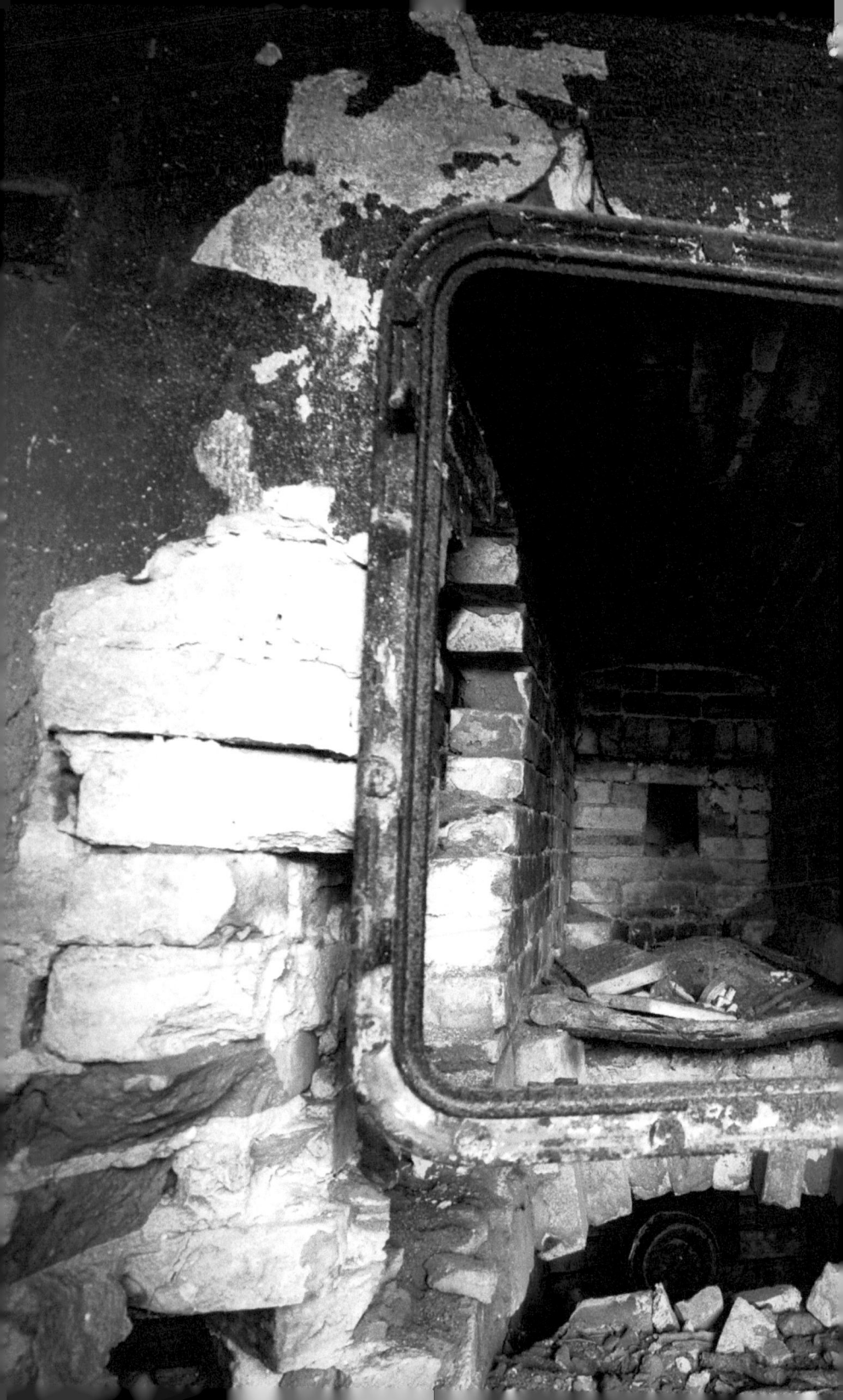

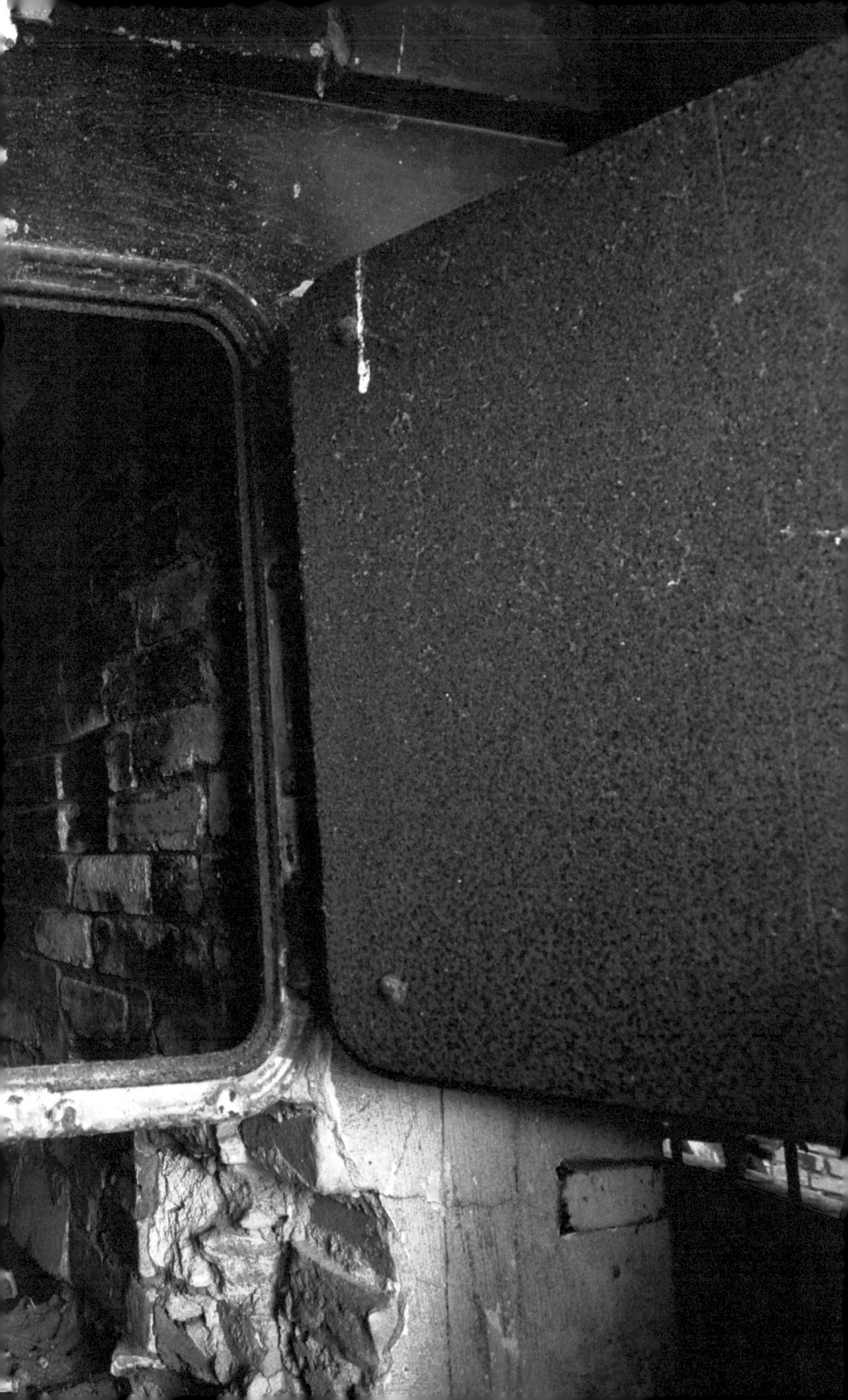

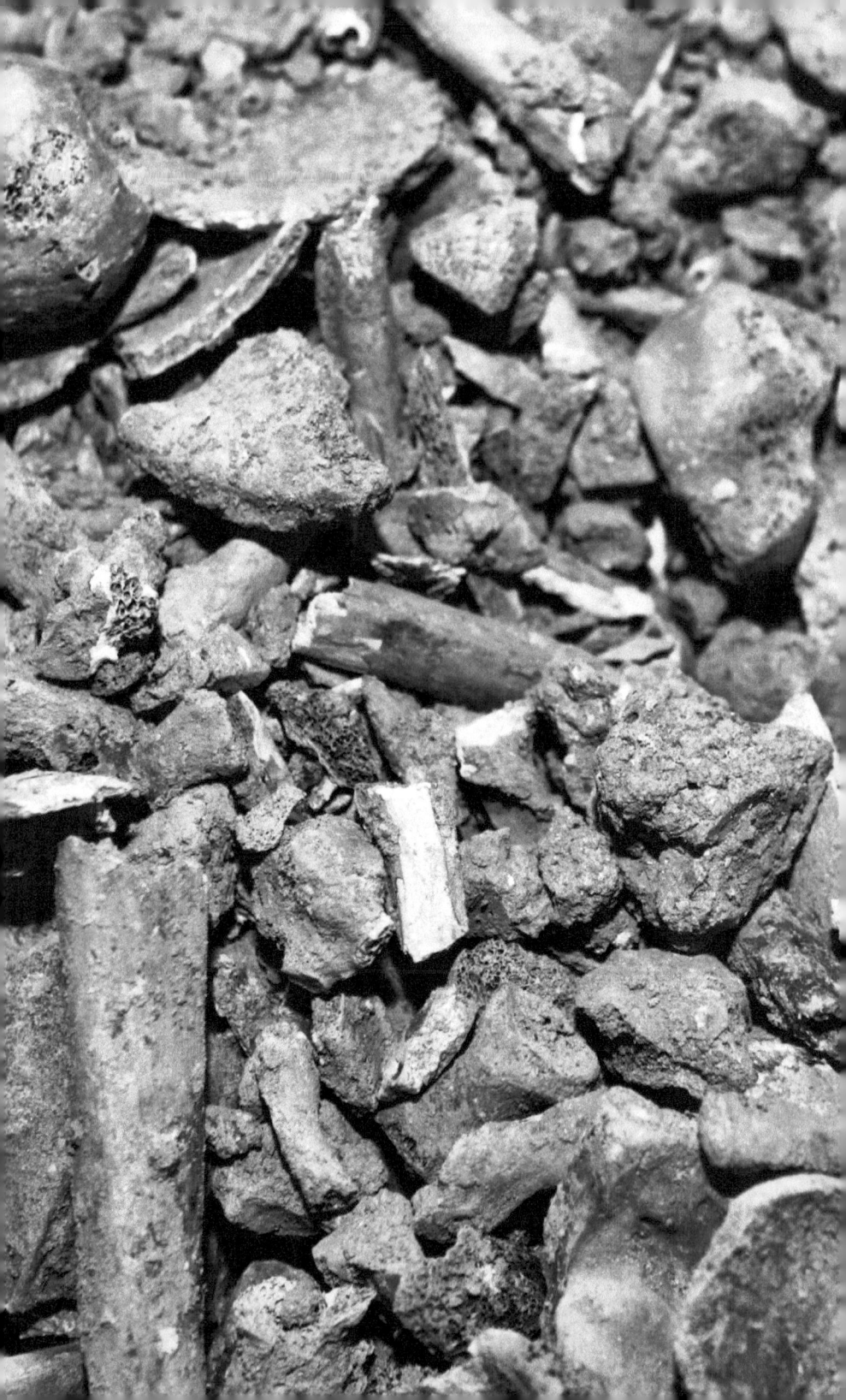

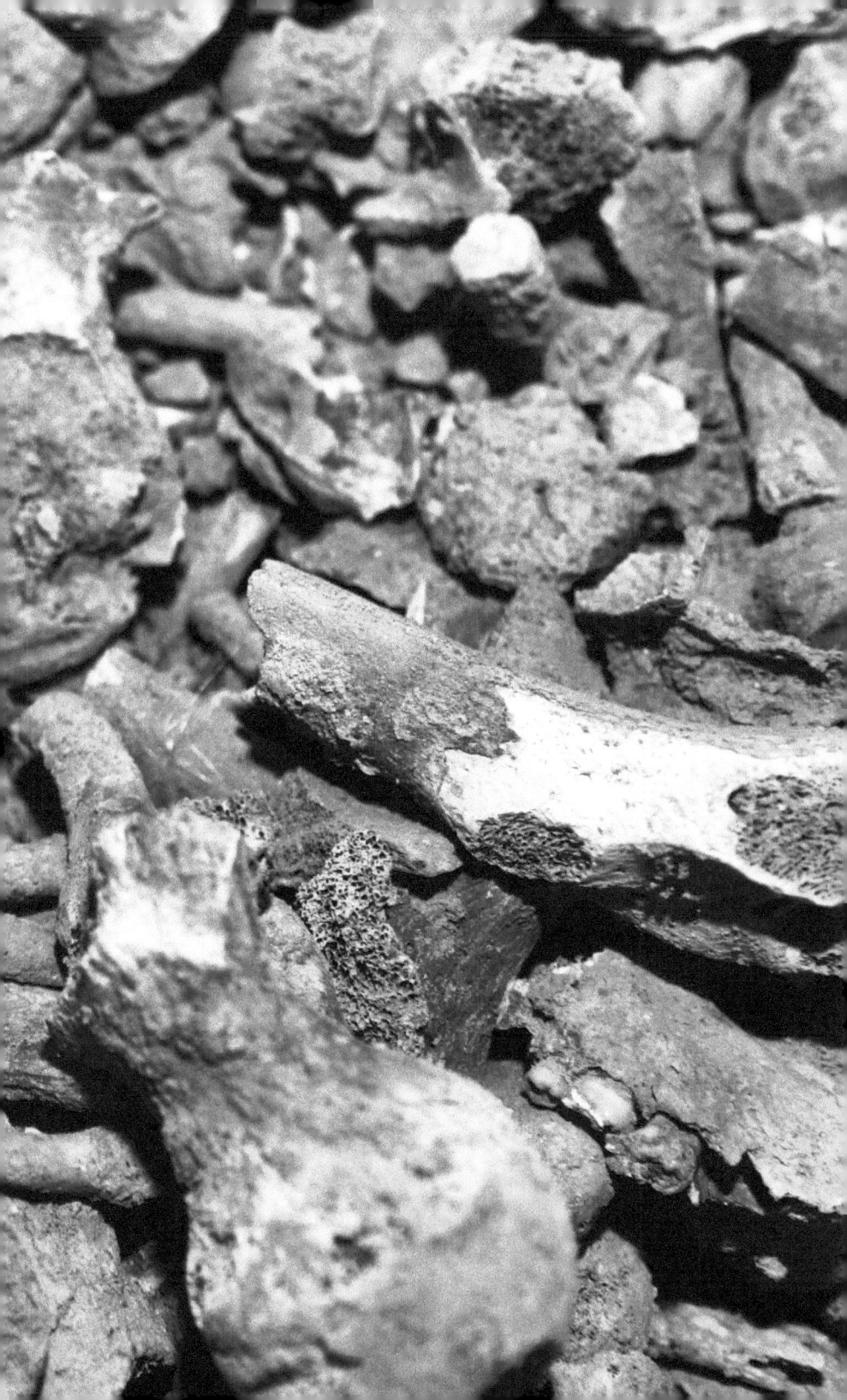

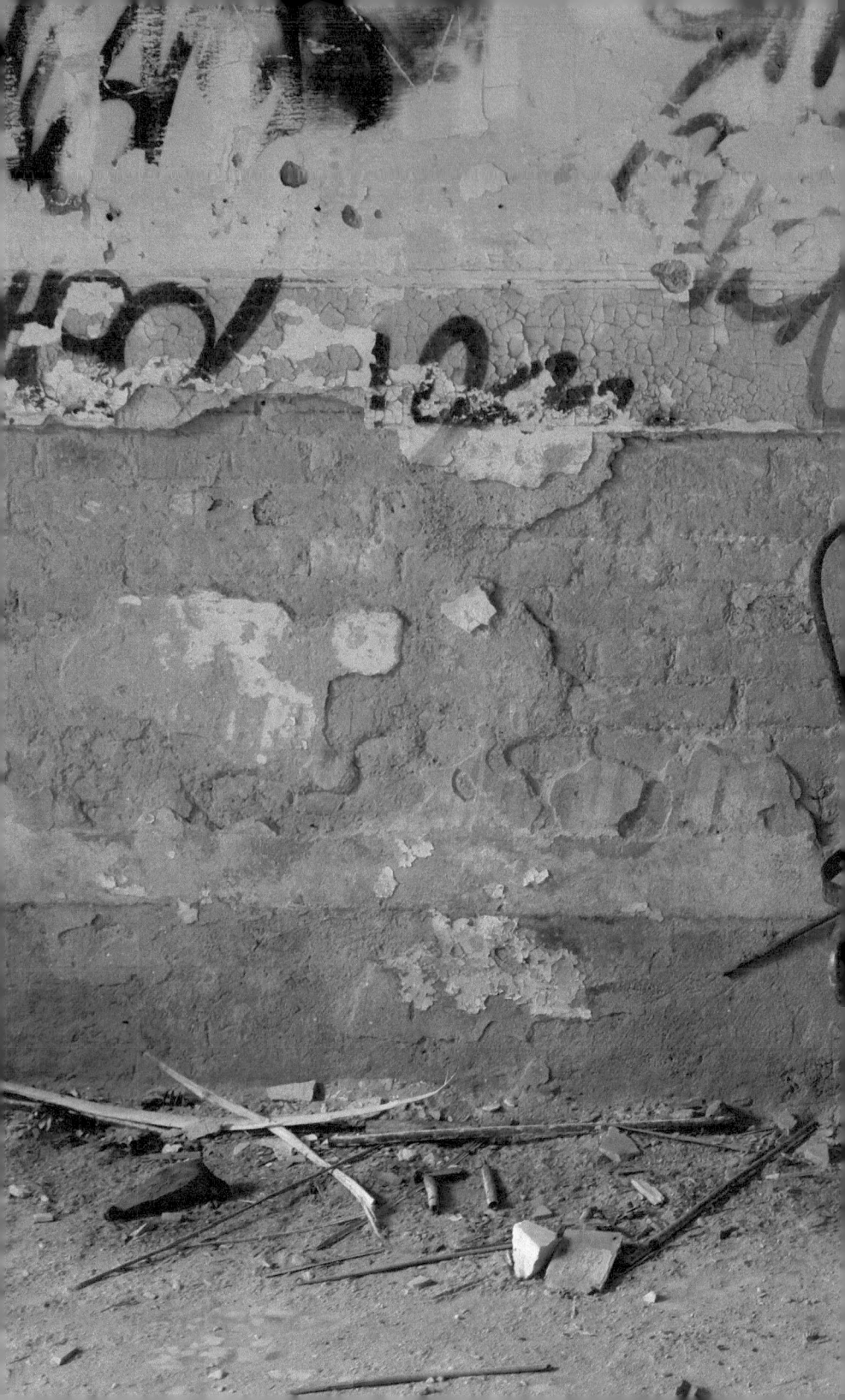

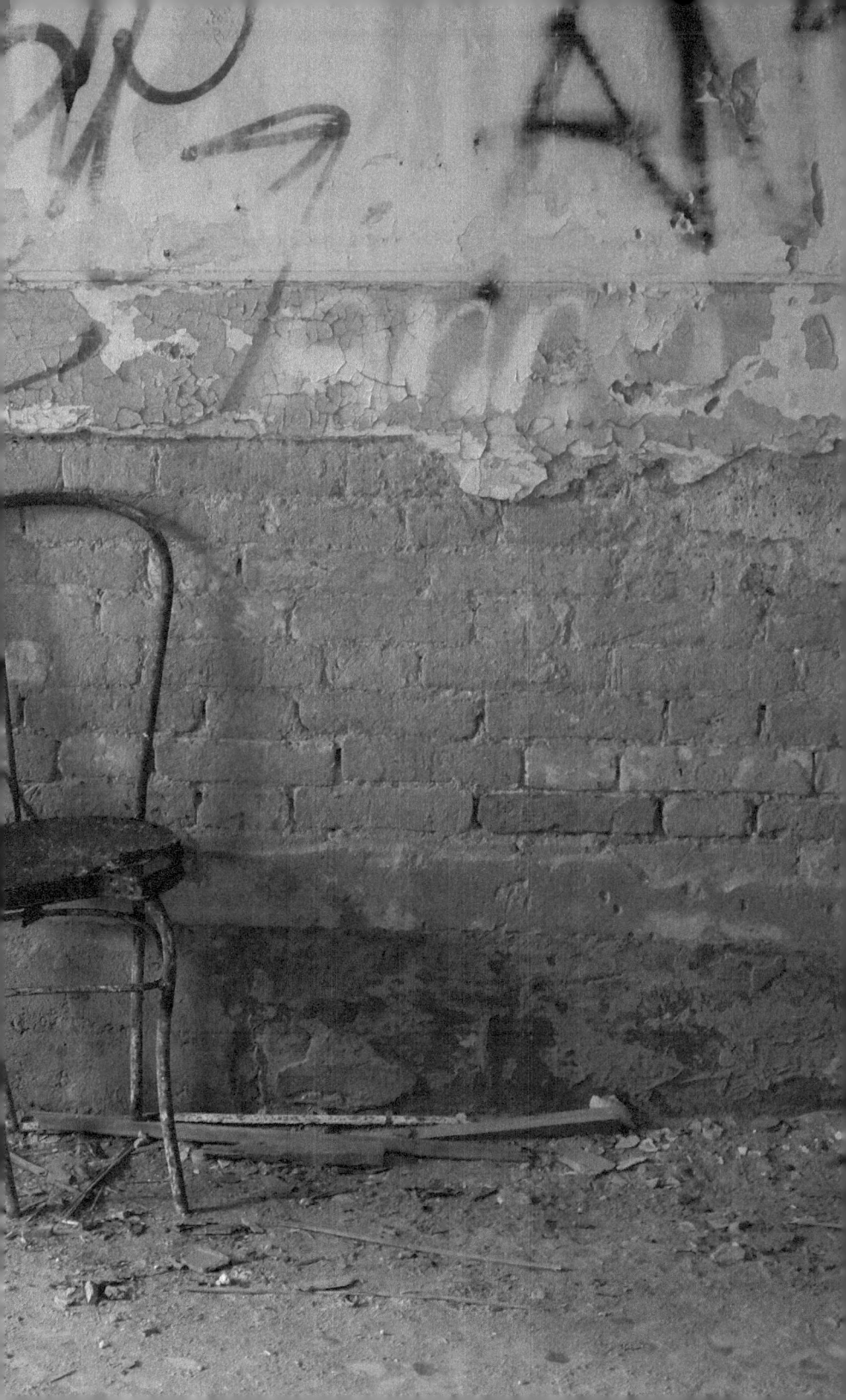

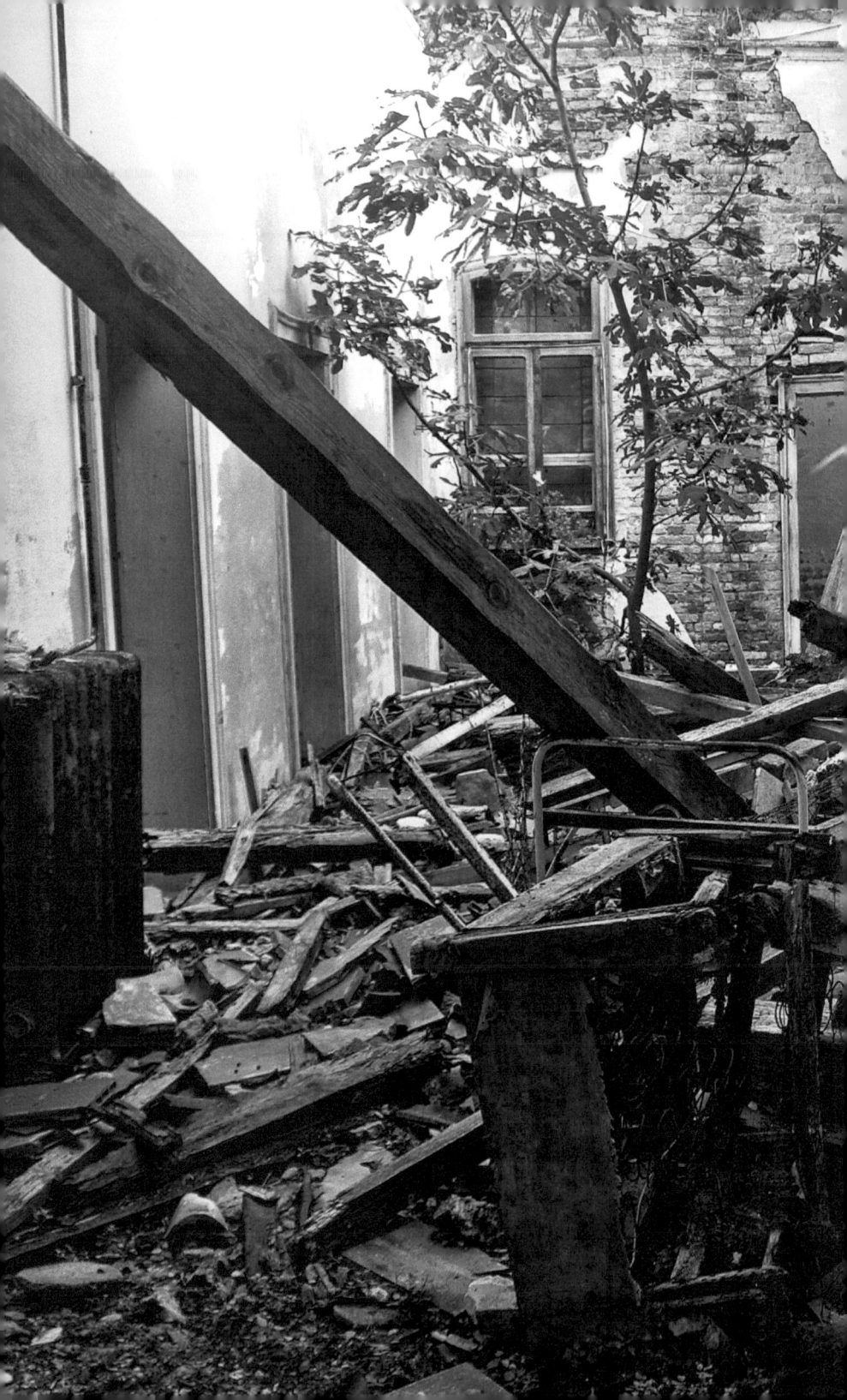

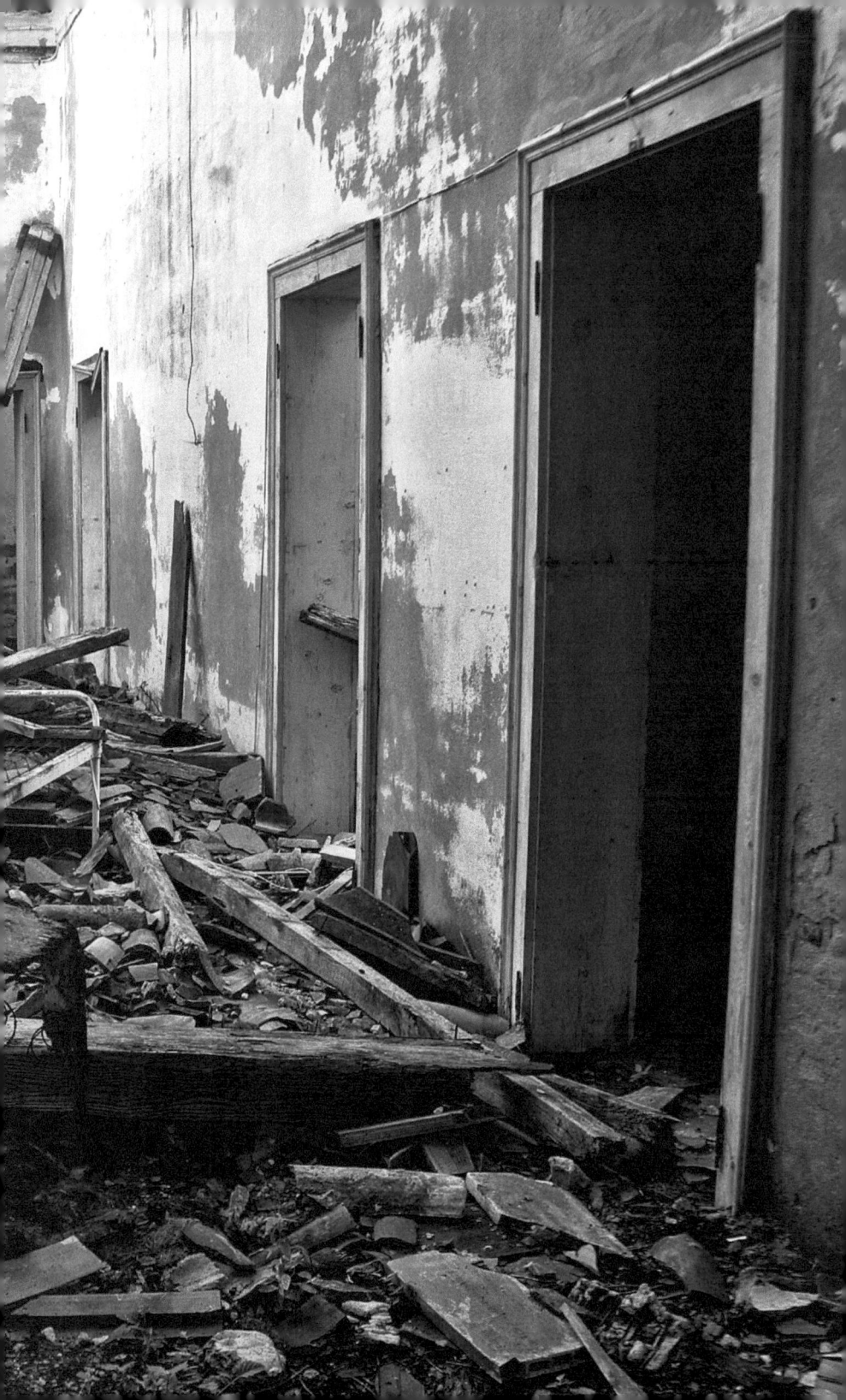

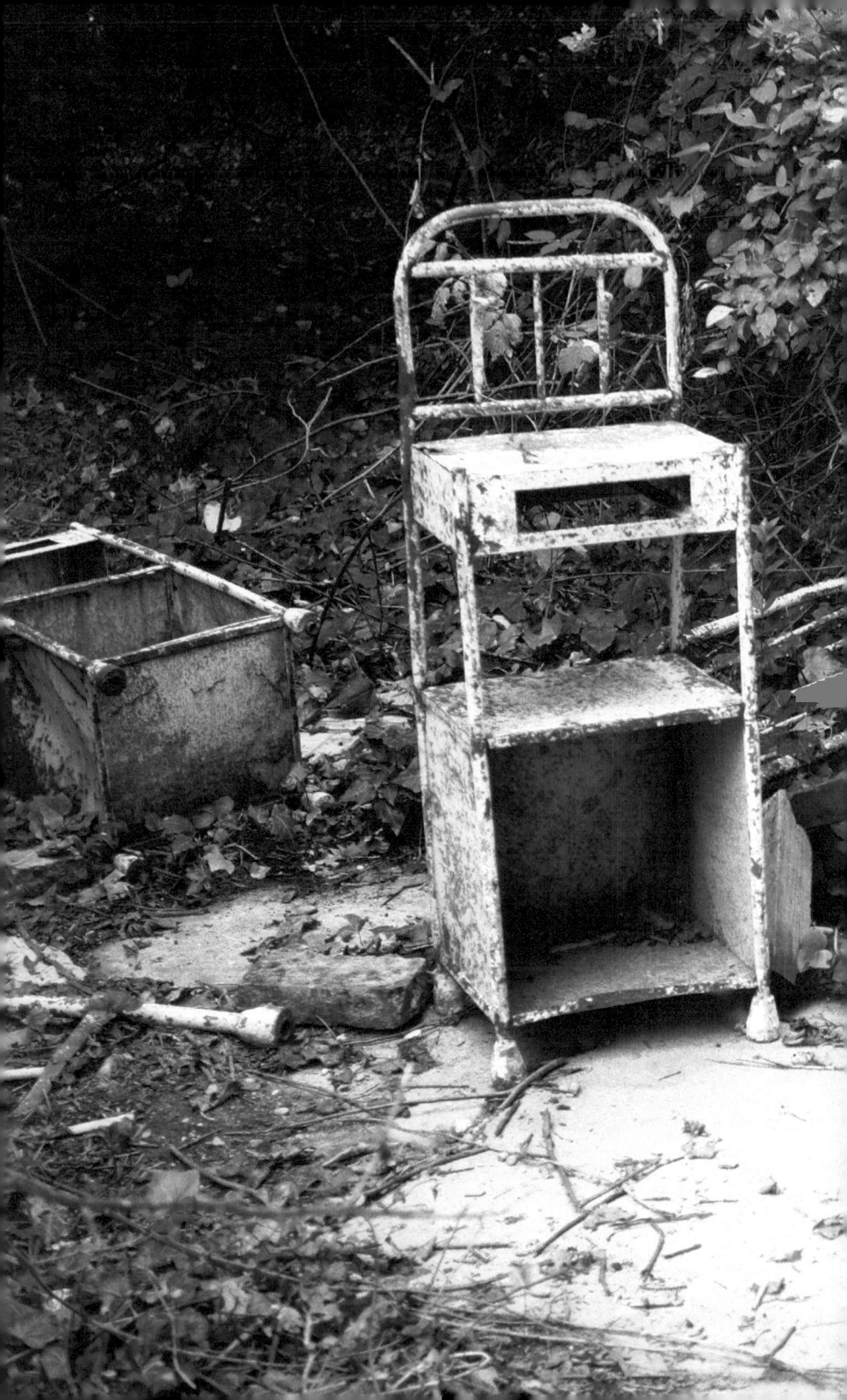

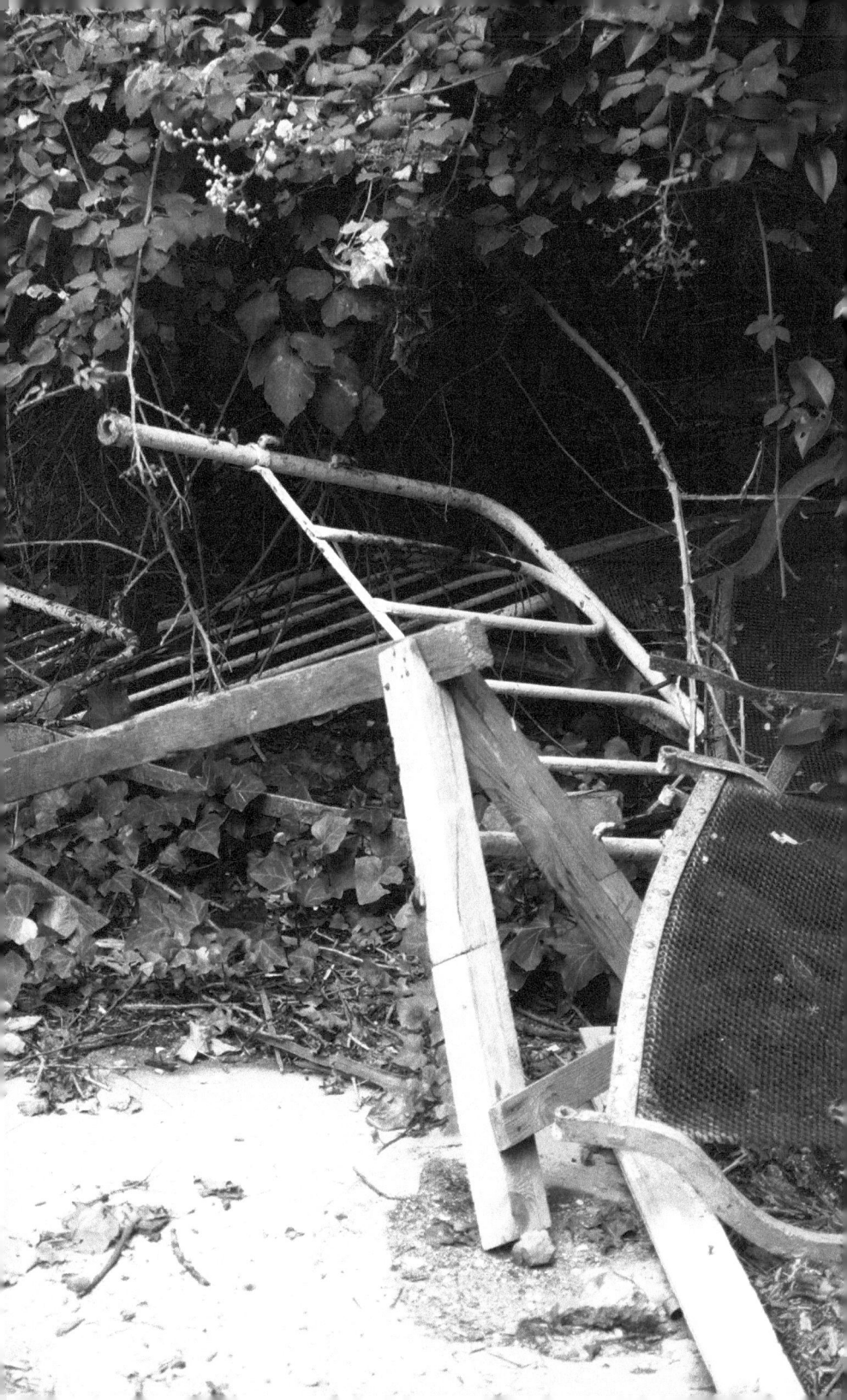

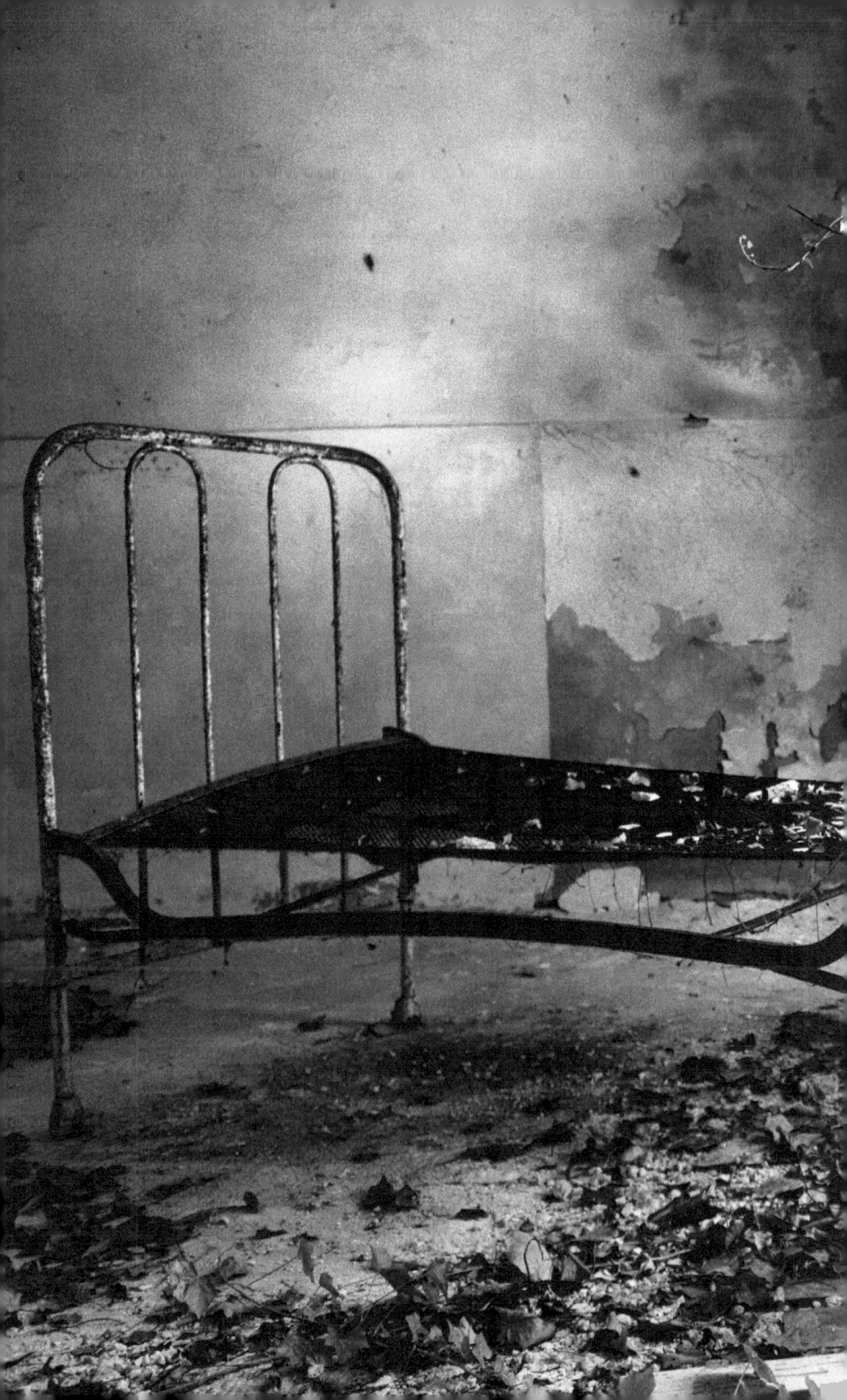

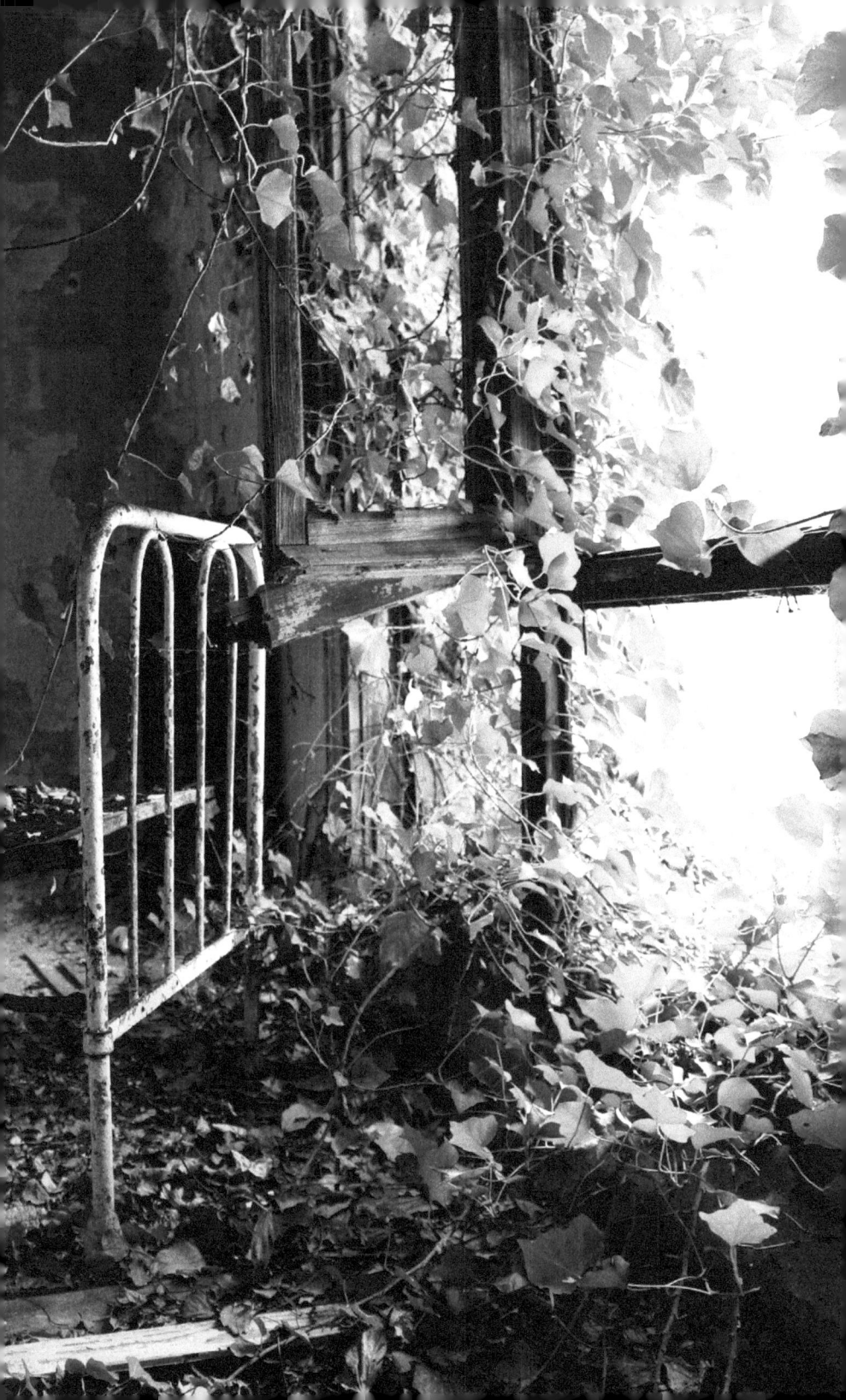

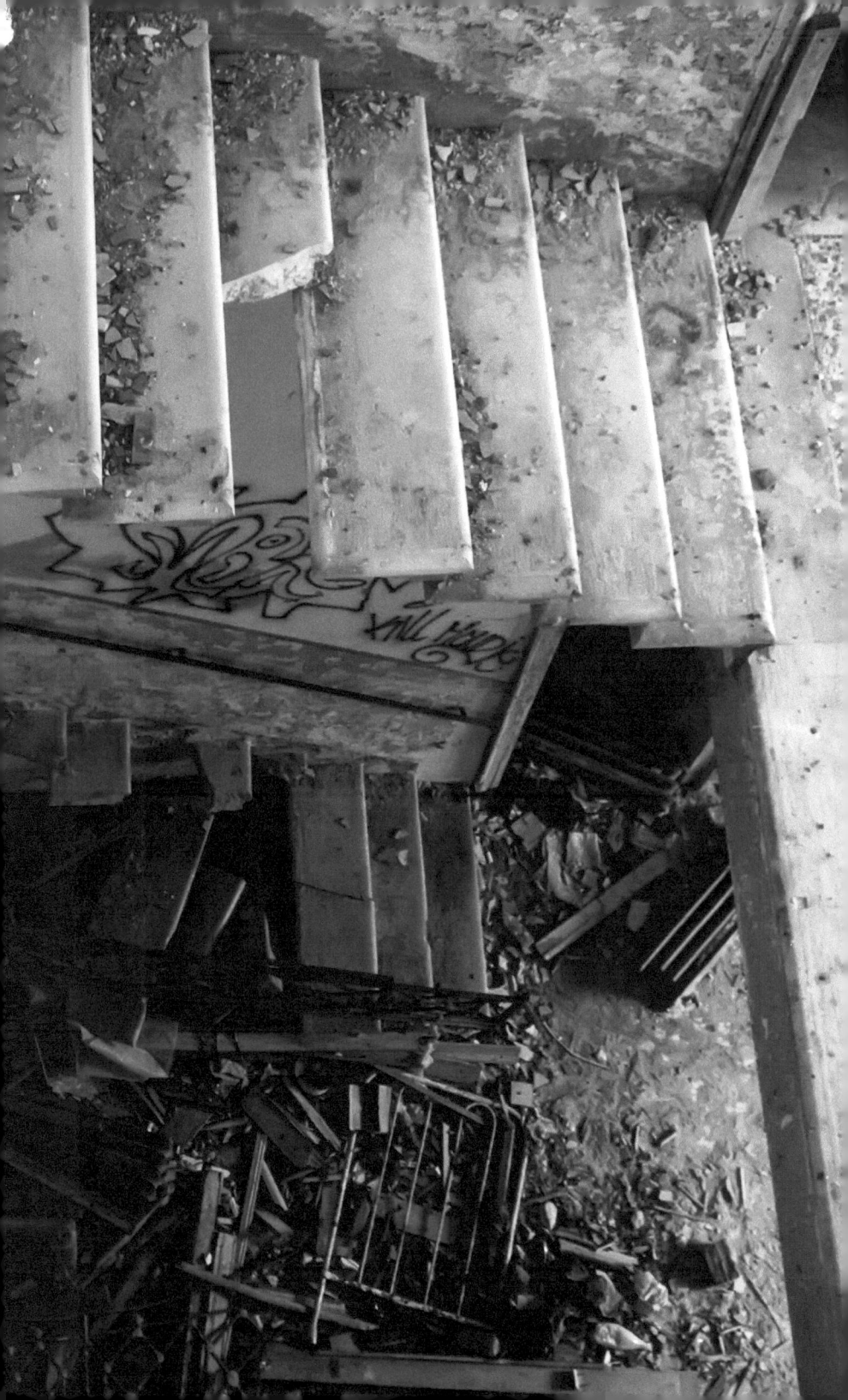

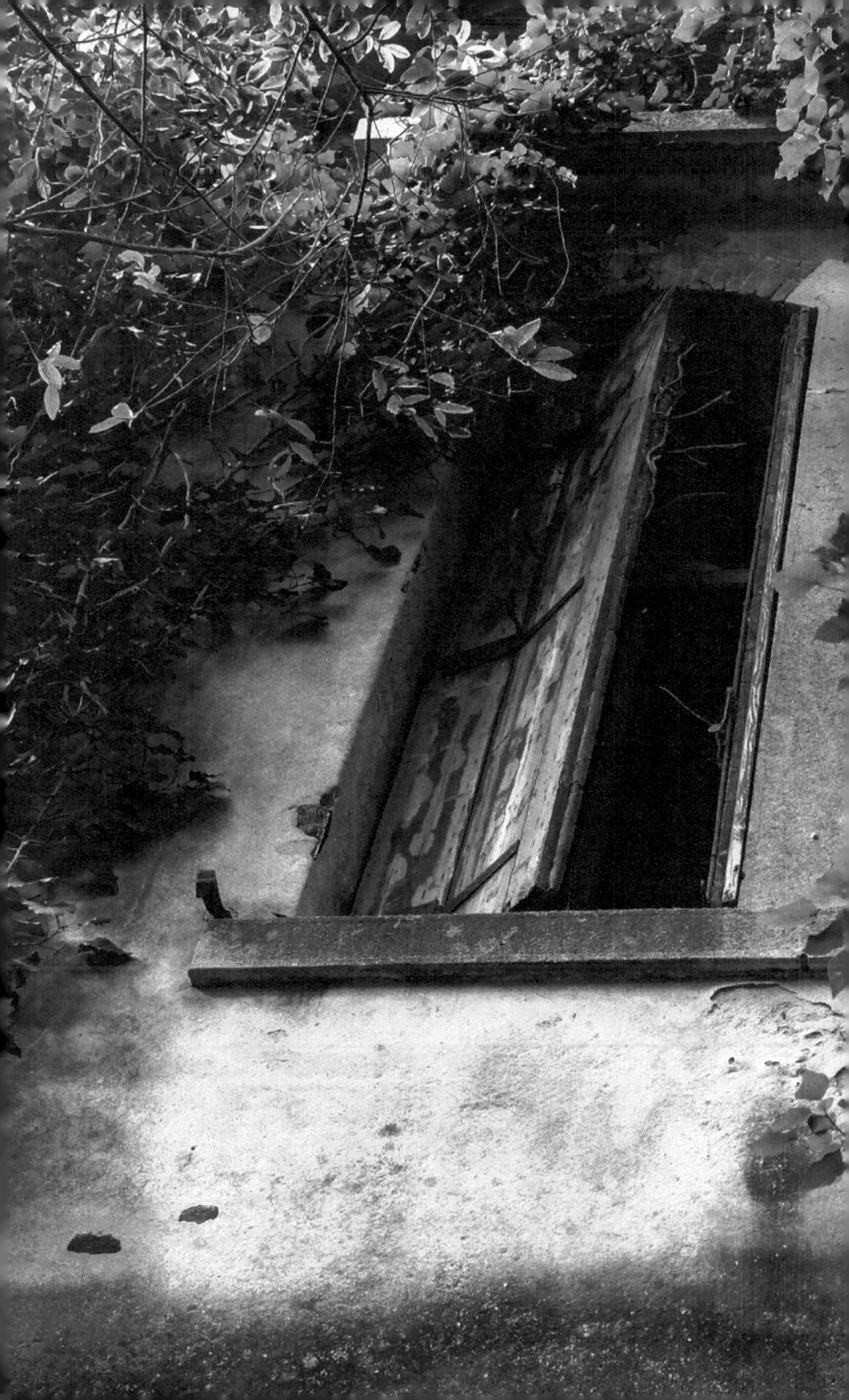

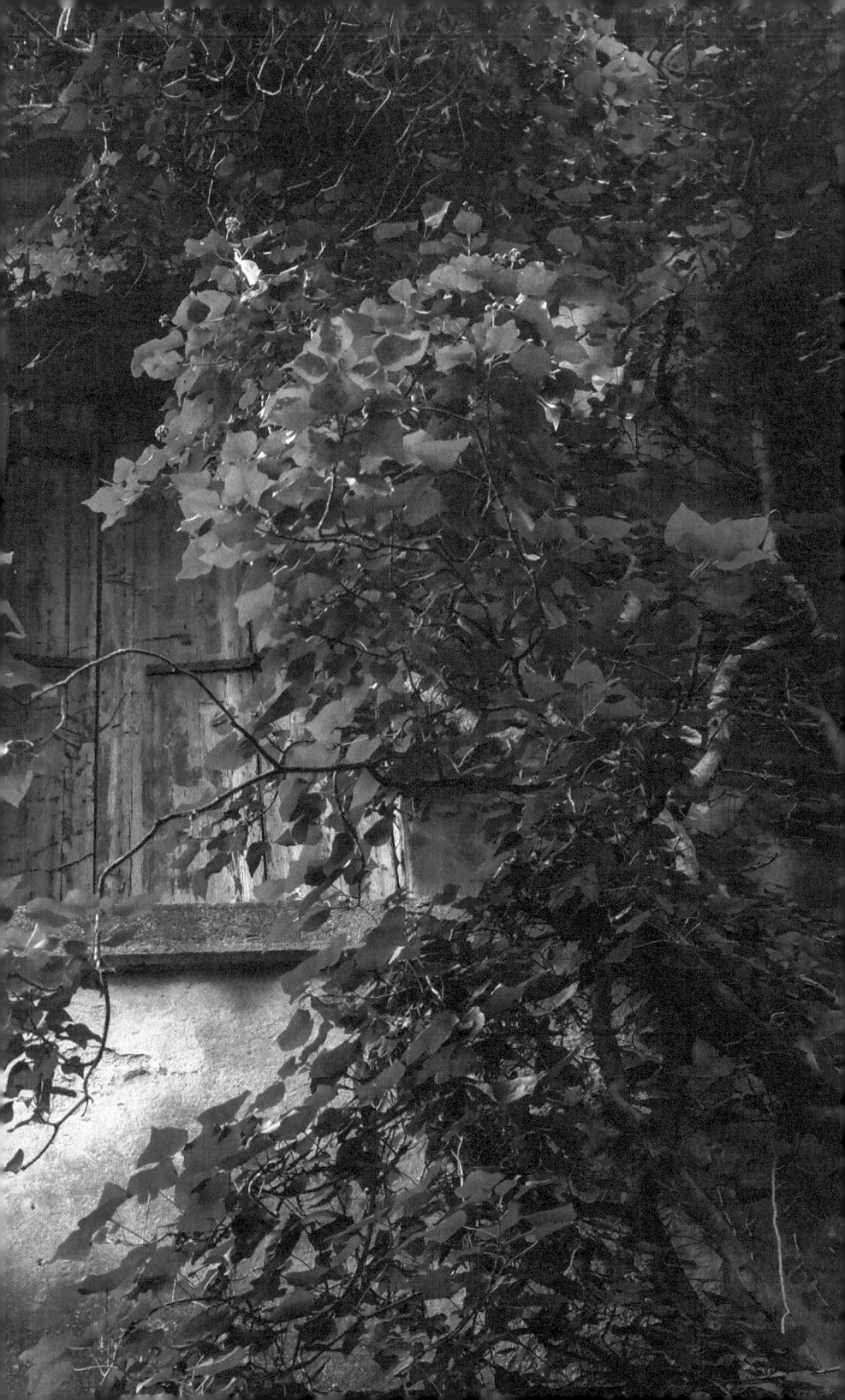

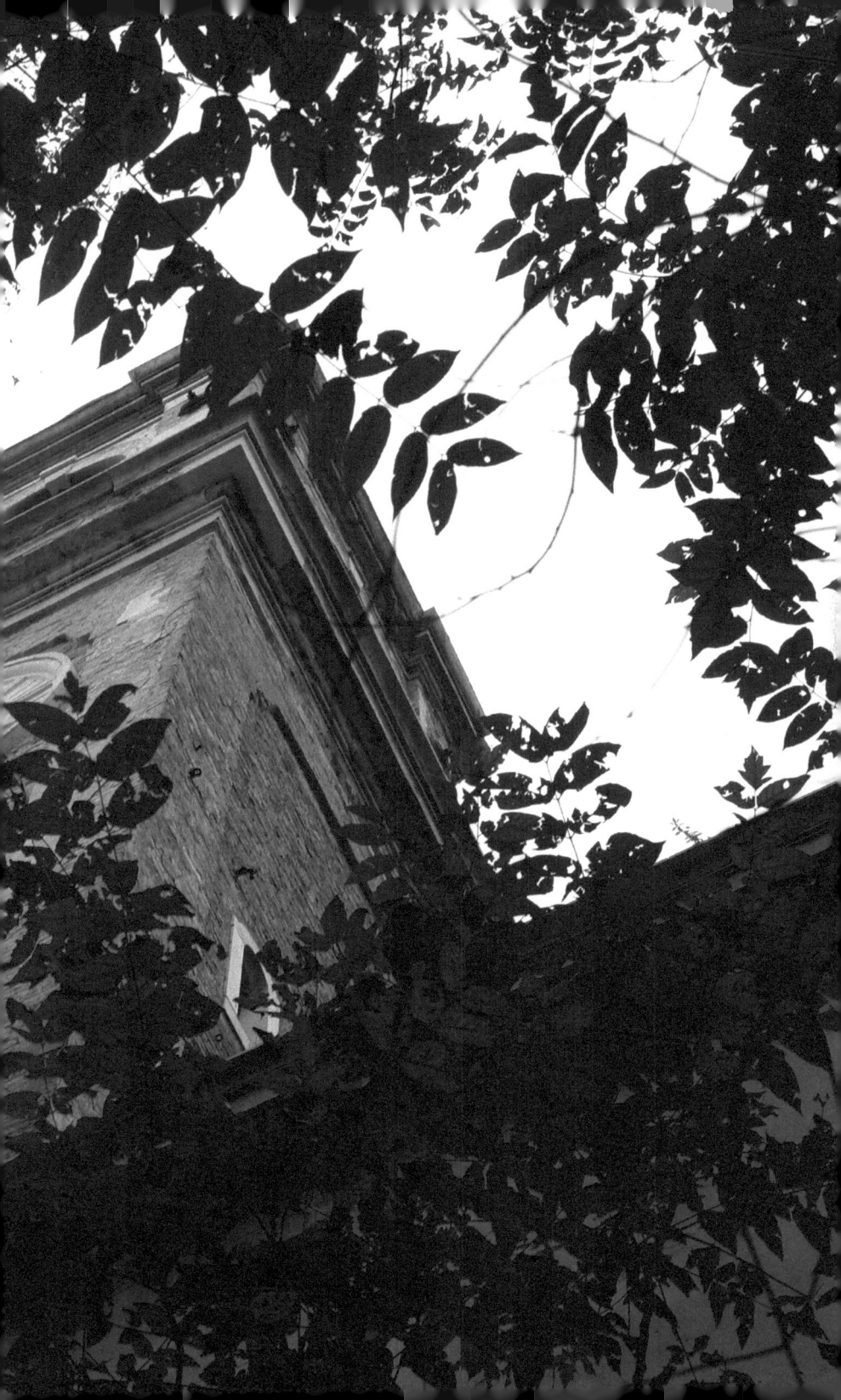

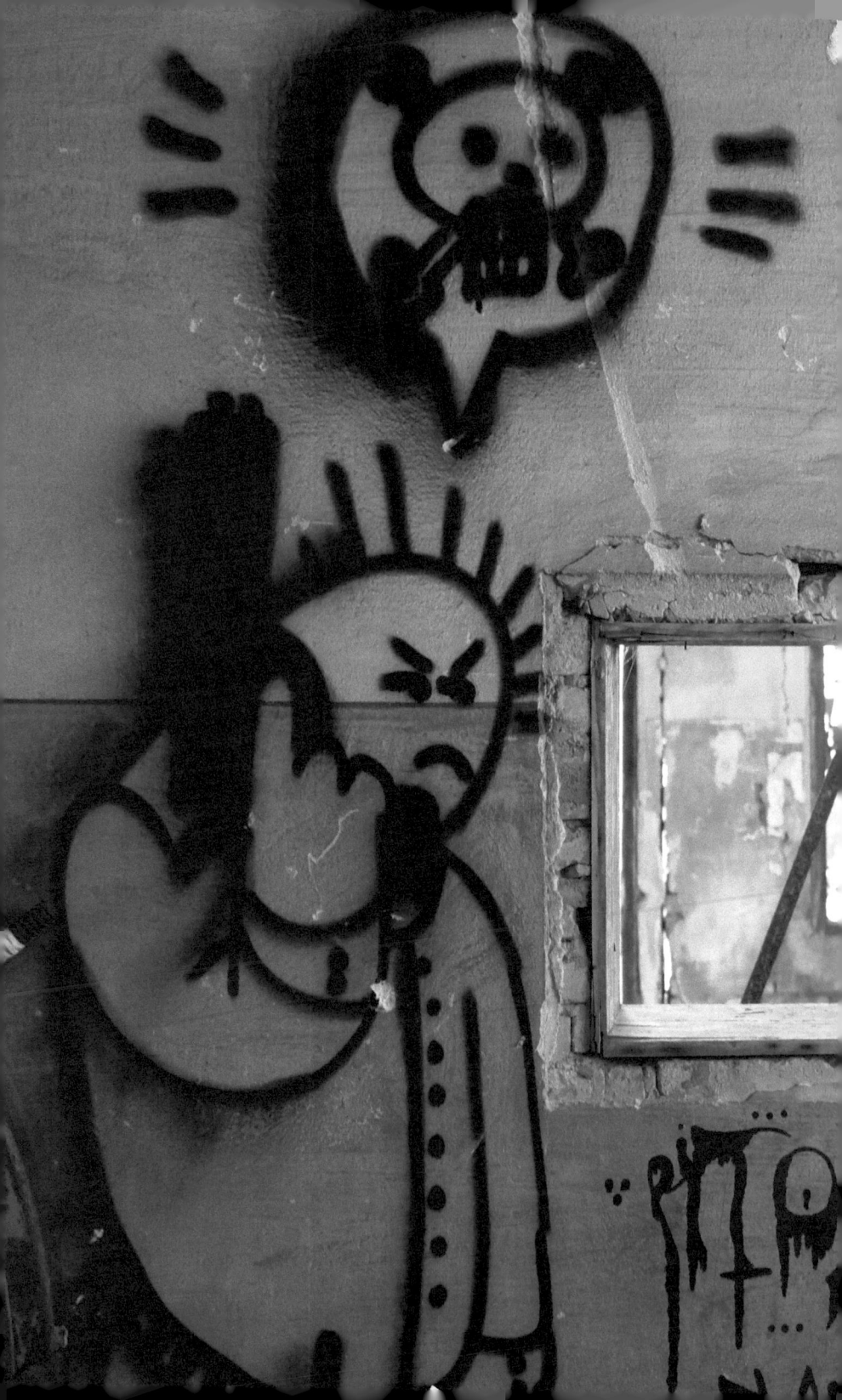

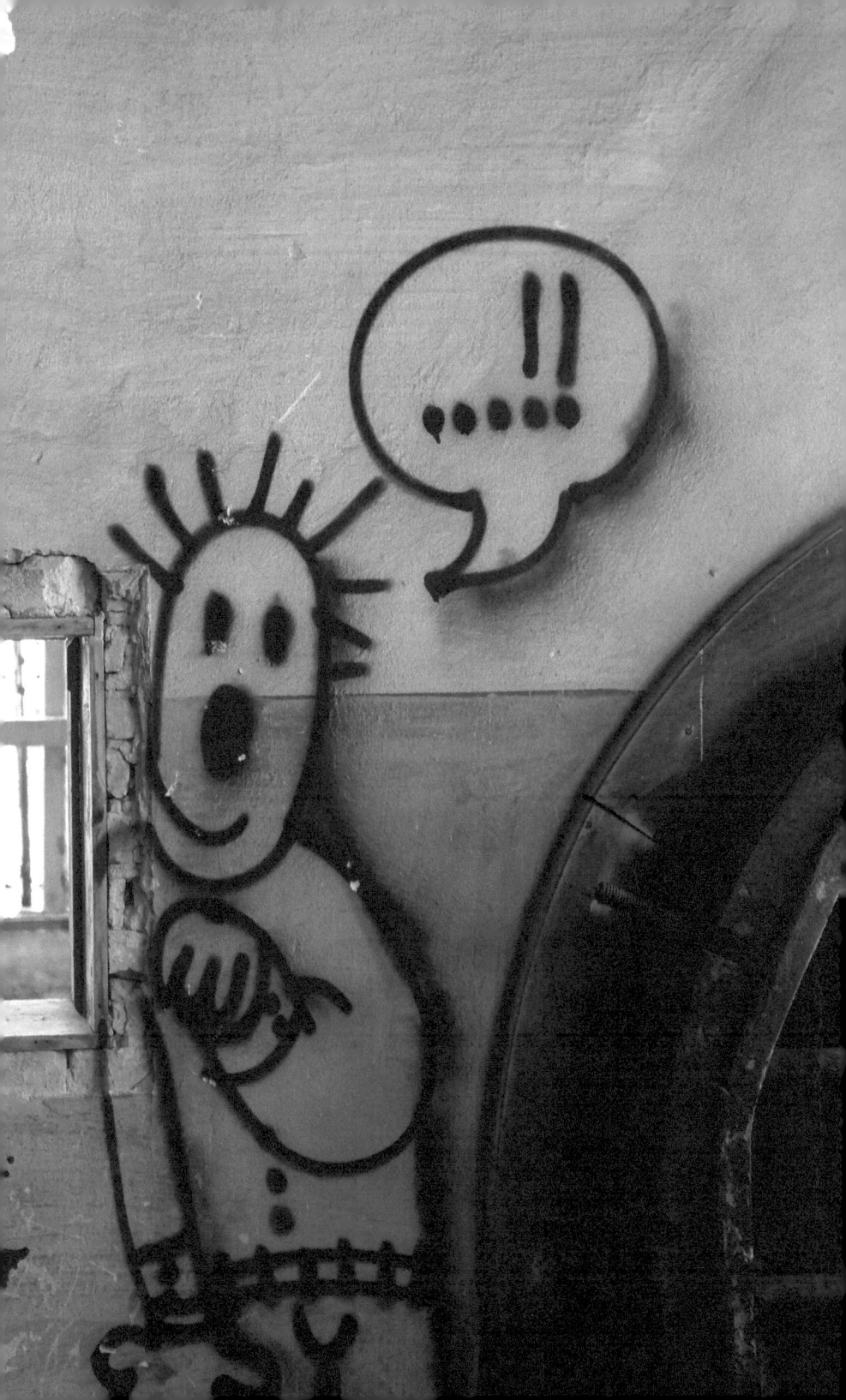

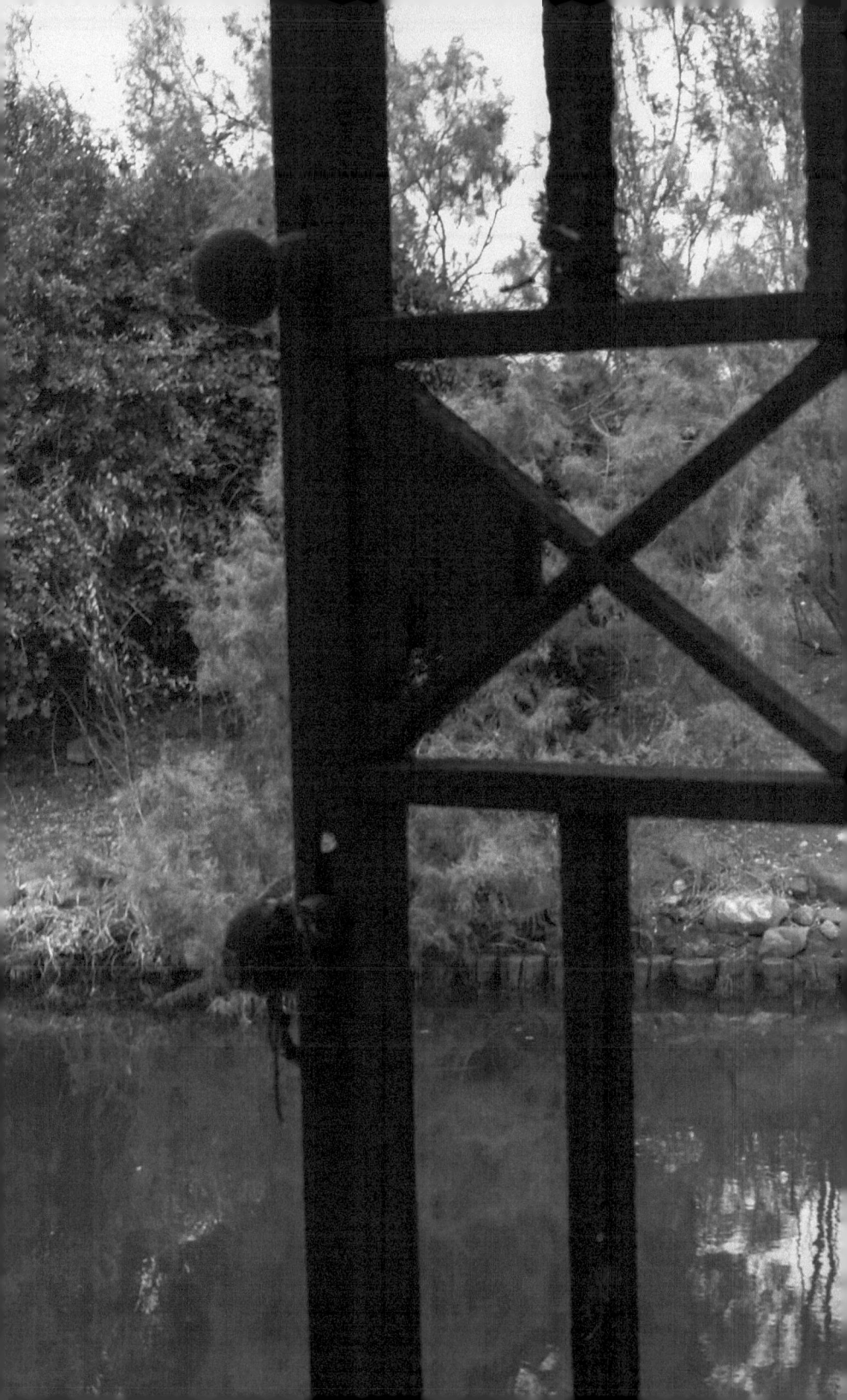

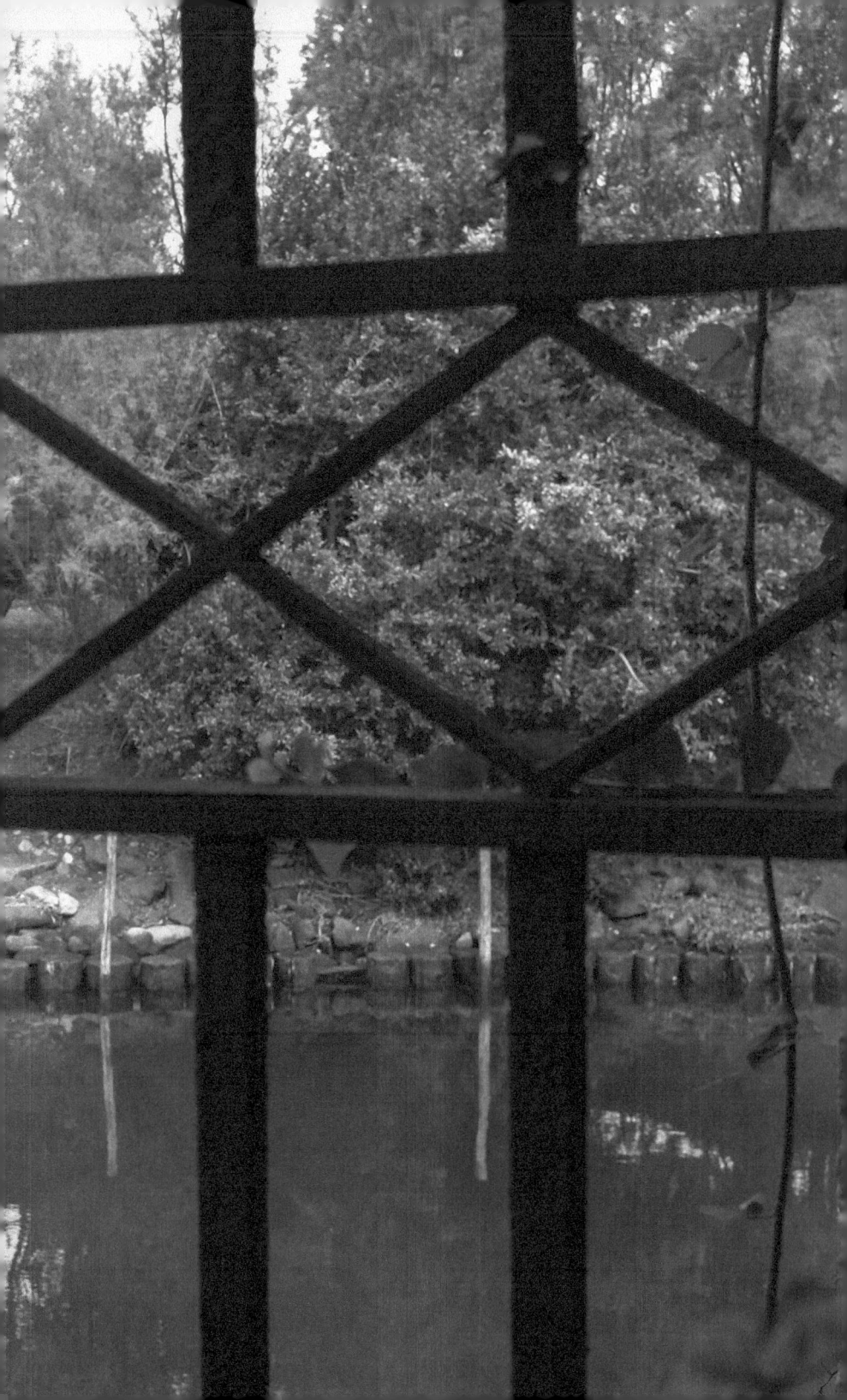

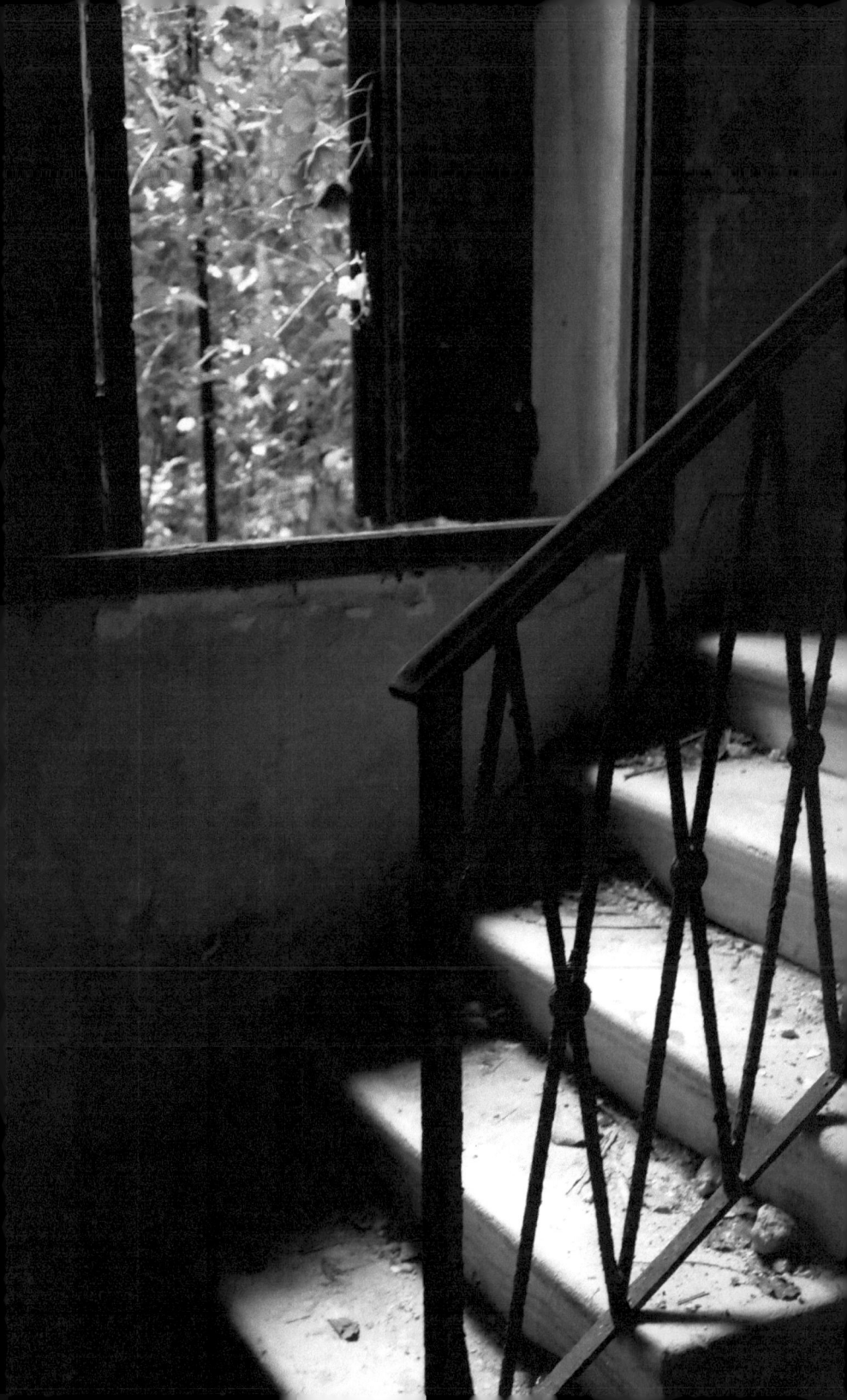

www.ingramcontent.com/pod-product-compliance
Lightning Source LLC
Chambersburg PA
CBHW040243220526
45473CB00001B/347